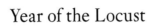

Year of the Locust

Ottoman Imperial Lancers, on parade near Jaffa Gate, Old City of Jerusalem, 1898. Courtesy Library of Congress, Eric Matson Collection.

Year of the Locust

A Soldier's Diary and the Erasure
of Palestine's Ottoman Past

Salim Tamari

UNIVERSITY OF CALIFORNIA PRESS

Berkeley   Los Angeles   London

University of California Press, one of the most distinguished university presses in the United States, enriches lives around the world by advancing scholarship in the humanities, social sciences, and natural sciences. Its activities are supported by the UC Press Foundation and by philanthropic contributions from individuals and institutions. For more information, visit www.ucpress.edu.

University of California Press
Berkeley and Los Angeles, California

University of California Press, Ltd.
London, England

Library of Congress Cataloging-in-Publication Data

Tamari, Salim.
    Year of the locust : a soldier's diary and the erasure of Palestine's Ottoman past / Salim Tamari.
        p. cm.
    Includes bibliographical references and index.
    ISBN 978-0-520-25955-3 (cloth : alk. paper)
    1. World War, 1914–1918—Palestine. 2. World War, 1914–1918—Jerusalem. 3. World War, 1914–1918—Campaigns—Middle East. 4. Turjman, Ihsan Hasan, 1893–1917—Diaries. 5. World War, 1914–1918—Personal narratives, Turkish. 6. Soldiers—Jerusalem—Diaries. 7. Turks—Jerusalem—Diaries. 8. Turkey. Ordu—History—World War, 1914–1918. 9. Jerusalem—History, Military—20th century. 10. Jerusalem—Social conditions—20th century. I. Title.
    D568.7.T36 2011
    940.4'15092—dc22
    [B]   2011004811

Manufactured in the United States of America

19   18
10   9   8   7   6   5   4   3   2

CONTENTS

FIGURES

ACKNOWLEDGMENTS

I am grateful to Rema Hammami, Irvin Schick, George Hintelian, Beshara Doumani, and Issam Nassar for their critical comments on an earlier draft. Ayşe Çavdar and Sibel Sayek helped me with Ottoman Turkish terms. Ayse was particularly helpful in locating old photographs and maps. I am also grateful to Khader Salameh for obtaining a copy of the manuscript diary and to Adil Mana and Abigail Jacobson for their helpful comments. Muhammad Ghosheh provided me with historical material on the al Salih/Turjman family from the Jerusalem Islamic Court records. Above all, I am indebted to Salih and Nabila Turjman, the grandchildren of Hasan Bey, and to Muhammad Khalidi in Amman, for their kindness in answering my endless questions on their family and for providing valuable records and family photographs. Baha Ju'beh took photos of the old Turjman house inside al Haram al Sharif. (A more extensive acknowledgment can be found in the Arabic introduction to the diaries, *'Am al-Jarad,* Institute for Palestine Studies, Beirut and Jerusalem,

2008.) My deep gratitude goes to Adrienne Harris for her great help in editing the final English draft, and to Niels Hooper, Nick Arrivo, and Suzanne Knott at the University of California Press for their considerable help, advice, and counseling in bringing this book to completion.

The Erasure of Ottoman Palestine

The past is a foreign country; they do things differently there.

Lesley Poles Hartley, *The Go-Between* (1953)

I fought the English troops at Gallipoli for an Ottoman country that no longer exists—even though I continued living on the same land.

Onbası (Umbashi) Muhammad Ali Awad, Palestinian officer in the Ottoman army from the village of Anabta who fought in Suez and in Gallipoli

Soldiers' diaries, particularly those from World War I, have been a constant reminder of the horrors of war. A large stock of such memoirs have reached us from the ranks of the Allied forces, particularly from British, French, American, and Anzac soldiers, as well as from Austrian and German soldiers fighting for the Central powers.[1] Much less material has been available from the Ottoman side, particularly from the Syrian provinces. This book analyzes the Great War from the perspective of three ordinary soldiers who fought on the Ottoman side, as expressed in the newly found diary of Private Ihsan Turjman and journal of Lieutenant Aref Shehadeh, both of Jerusalem, as well as in the published Turkish diary of Mehmet (Muhammad) Fasih of Mersin. It explores two important ways in which the Great War impacted the Ottoman Empire. First, it examines how the experience of the war transformed the consciousness and the living conditions of the people of the Arab East (Ottoman Syria)—a shift that historians sometimes describe as the onset of Arab modernity. Second, it looks at what Falih Rıfkı, the Ottoman essayist and modernist, called—with the benefit of hindsight—the "Turkish problem" in Syria: namely the inability of Ottoman constitutional reform to create a multiethnic domain in which the Syria (including Palestine) would become an integral part of the empire. The crucial time for both these transformations was the short but critical six-year period between the constitutional revolution of 1908, with its project for a representative, multi-

3

ethnic state, and the collapse of this project under the dictatorial regime of Cemal Pasha.

While the events discussed in the diary in the second part of this book center in the city of Jerusalem and show the war's impact on the urban population, they also had a significant impact on the region as a whole. Jerusalem, we have to remember, was the administrative and political center of a huge Ottoman province, the Mutasarflik of al Quds al Sharif, which comprised more than half of what became Mandate Palestine. Its *ashraf* and notables were a critical elite with a major influence on Ottoman policy in Istanbul as well as in Jaffa, Hebron, and other regional centers.[2] The devastation felt by the city during the war—food shortages, disease, pauperization, and mass deportation—was repeated throughout the region in various degrees. The city was the crucible in which the breakdown in the normative system, and the subsequent rupture with the region's Ottoman past, was first experienced; from there, the turmoil engulfed the rest of the country.

The hero of our story is Ihsan Hasan Turjman (1893–1917), a common soldier in the Ottoman military headquarters in Jerusalem. His life was short and uneventful—he served as a clerk in the Manzil (Commissariat) and briefly as a foot soldier in Nablus and Hebron—but his observations on the impact of military events on his relationship to his city and his nation are without parallel. The power of wartime diaries lies in their exposure of the texture of daily life, long buried in the political rhetoric of nationalist discourse, and in their restoration of a world that has been hidden by subsequent denigration of the Ottoman past— the life of communitarian alleys, obliterated neighborhoods, heated political debates projecting possibilities that no longer exist, and the voices of street actors silenced by elite memoirs:

soldiers, peddlers, prostitutes, and vagabonds. By the third year of the war, the diaries of such ordinary soldiers project a desperate search for *normalcy* in daily life—a normalcy that was experienced in prewar Ottoman Palestine but seemed to elude its citizens for the next hundred years.

The Great War brought about a radical break with the Ottoman past in the whole Arab East, not only in the established constitutional regime but also in the system of governance, local administration, and identity politics. In the popular memory of peasants and city folk alike, 1915 was the Year of the Locust (*'am al Jarad*). Even four generations later, the locust invasion continues to evoke the combined memory of natural disasters and the manmade devastation of war. These events erased four centuries of a rich and complex Ottoman patrimony in which popular narratives of war and nationalist ideology colluded. An anti-Ottoman rewriting of history took place simultaneously, and in the same abrupt manner, both on the Turkish side (in the guise of modernizing the state and making it geographically manageable) and on the Arab side (in the sustained annals of nationalist historiography). The erasure replaced four centuries of relative peace and dynamic activity, the Ottoman era, with what was known in Arabic discourse as "the days of the Turks": four miserable years of tyranny symbolized by the military dictatorship of Ahmad Cemal Pasha in Syria, *seferberlik* (forced conscription and exile), and the collective hanging of Arab patriots in Beirut's Burj Square on August 15, 1916.

This book deals with the totalizing and transformative nature of the Great War. The war was *totalizing* not only in the manner in which it molded soldiers' work and living habits but also in its impact on the daily lives of civilians, creating an atmosphere of continued panic and uncertainty and disrupting daily patterns

Figure 1. Dead Ottoman soldier holding a hand grenade, Sheikh Jarrah, Jerusalem, December 1917. Courtesy Library of Congress, Eric Matson Collection.

of behavior. This anxiety often took the form of persistent concern about food, clothing, and the availability of essential commodities such as kerosene and tobacco, as well as fear of arbitrary army actions (arrest, transfer of populations, and conscription of older people as the war progressed). This period also saw the first systematic censorship of the press and of people's private mail. In a related process, the Great War had transformative effects on social norms. In the absence of adult male household members—who either were conscripted or perished at the front—many families suffered extreme poverty, famine, and disease. People were driven to drastic measures that undermined traditional normative behavior. Begging, theft, and prostitution became daily features in the streets of Jerusalem. The war ultimately helped redefine the nature of the state and its relationship to its subjects. In Palestine the war was a watershed that separated the country from its Syrian expanses and brought British colonial rule, creating new borders, new citizenship, and new forms of national consciousness.

The war also had an unanticipated emancipatory impact on society. This aspect is not well discussed in war literature, which stresses rather its devastation, dehumanization, and disruption of normality. Yet in many respects it was precisely the instruments of brutalization and destruction—and particularly the disruption of normalcy—that opened up new social horizons. For example, the socialist theoretician Anton Pannekoek has argued that World War I played a crucial role in shedding illusions about nationalism and opening possibilities for class solidarities across national boundaries.[3] In the aftermath of the Franco-Prussian war of 1870, Engels made a similar analysis of the impact of a future "total war" in which barbarism would give rise to a new civilization.[4] In the same vein, the movement of large numbers of young males from rural areas to army camps created a network of training grounds for former peasants in literacy and manual skills that laid the foundation for mass movements and radical reform. In Palestine and the Syrian provinces of the Ottoman regime, the war had the opposite effect on nationalism and national boundaries. It decisively undermined progress toward a multinational, multiethnic state and gave rise to narrow and exclusivist nationalist ideologies and provincial affinities. But as in Europe it brought masses of people into greater contact with their national communities and enabled the wider introduction of literacy, as well as the expansion of transport networks and greater electrification in urban society—a process that had already been set in motion by the Ottoman reforms of the 1850s but now accelerated several fold.

The presence of army camps near major towns catalyzed many of these changes. Khalid Fahmy has examined the conflictual modernity brought about by Muhammad Ali's army on nineteenth-century Egypt.[5] This process of massive military socialization came to Palestine several decades later, especially after the conscription act of 1914. The first segments of the population to experience the impact of this mobilization were peasants and small-town conscripts. In the Arab East, as in mid-nineteenth-century Egypt, local society underwent changes that altered the rural landscape and redefined its relationship to the city. In his major study of the criminal underworld in World War I Alexandria, *The Men of Raya and Sekina,* Salah Issa examines the world created by the labor battalions—a sort of conscript peasant labor force created by the British administration, the exact equivalent of the Ottoman *Tawabeer al 'amaleh* (labor battalions; *amele taburları* in Turkish) described in Ihsan Turjman's diary of his war years in Palestine.[6]

These conscript "volunteer labor battalions"—essentially compulsory work gangs—were crucial instruments in building projects, assigned to build roads, railroad tracks, army encampments, and military installations. The misery of these conscripts, often sent to die in the distant expanses of Anatolia or in Gallipoli or the Sinai desert, was tempered by a salutary side: they were offered free food, lodging, and (sometimes) relocation to the big cities of the empire. These forced "volunteers" had almost no option but to join the army. The alternative was often death by starvation. Moreover, the conscripts, isolated in their camp life, developed a critical distance from the normative ethics of their original communities when they moved to the margins of major cities like Alexandria and Cairo.

> Since one of their major tasks was to remove the dead and the injured from the battlefield, they became used to the sight of blood and war casualties. They became immune to death, and the mass carnage of war. The ethical norms of civilian life, and the communal boundaries of behaviour from which they had originally come, no longer restrained them in an atmosphere in which killing the enemy became a primary target.[7]

The conscripts also became used to new patterns of consumption and behavior, which created a further rupture from their earlier habitat:

> They became attuned to life in the big city, in which they created the illusion that it was their last port of migration; one that would realize their dream of a more hopeful life than the life of village drudgery they came from. . . . They became used to a cycle of disciplined work, and experienced the luxury of three meals a day, of consuming meat, and buqsumat (army biscuits) and jam—and of periodic changing of their clothes with clean attire. War gave them the opportunity to meet men from other regions which they had

only heard about, and to travel in open markets and city boulevards which they had not dreamt of seeing before.[8]

Above all, these experiences of war made it difficult for these conscripts to go back to their villages and towns, and made them shed what Issa calls "the virtue of contentment" typical among Turkish and Arab peasants. Upon their release, this "loss of contentment," among other things, created the social background for the criminal underworld that haunted Alexandria and other port cities of the Mediterranean in the postwar period.

In Palestine the war transformed the country into one major construction site. The Syrian and Palestinian labor battalions *(Tawabeer al 'amaleh)* were mobilized by the Ottoman Corps of Army Engineers to substantially modernize the communication and transportation system.[9] Many features of Palestine's modernity that have been attributed to the British colonial administration seem to have been initiated by the Ottomans in this period. In the first modern history of Palestine in the new century (published in 1920), Khalil Totah and Omar Salih Barghouti discussed the major changes brought about by the technological exigencies of war. Water wells were drilled all over the country and linked through pipes to the major urban centers. Railroads linked the northern part of the country to the southern front; a network of telephones and telegraph lines connected the country to the outside world. Post offices, which originated in consular European services, were unified and replaced by the Ottoman postal services; roads were expanded to allow the passage of military traffic and mechanized cars (automobiles and buses).[10] Public hospitals, clinics, and pharmacies were introduced in all provinces to combat the malaria, cholera, and typhus epidemics during the war. urban poor. The labor battalions that built this infrastructure—recruited from released prisoners, village dwellers (chosen by lottery), and the urban poor—were different from the conscripts in the army *(nizamiyyeh)*, who undertook the brunt of the fighting on the front and from whose ranks emerged the two diaries I discuss below.[11]

Nevertheless, the emancipatory features of war affected both the regulars and the "volunteers" (because the latter often belonged to minority groups, the Ottomans deemed them unreliable for the front). They both experienced army discipline in military camps, were uprooted from their traditional communities, and traveled throughout the empire for the first time; and both came in contact with "ethnic others" in the imperial army: Turks, Kurds, Syrians, Albanians, and Bulgarians, as well as Austrian and German officers from the European Allies.

The war period also witnessed substantial transformations of lifestyles and work habits. Pocket watches were now worn by the urban population and regulated the beginning and end of work days. Men increasingly met in coffeehouses rather than in each other's homes. An increasing number of middle-class women removed their veils, joined the workforce, and participated in the emerging secular public culture. In Jerusalem and Jaffa (as in Beirut, Aleppo, and Damascus) nightclubs and bordellos became available to members of the armed forces under the regulation of the state.[12] In their history of turn-of-the-century Palestine, Totah and Barghouti observe the beneficial interaction between the civilians and the military, and the impact of travel to Beirut, Damascus, and Aleppo on people from small towns. But they also lament the decline of the old moral order when people were exposed to the "degenerate" influences of army life:

> During the war we witnessed the spread of social diseases among city folks, and we thought that this was a national product [of the war]. But when the German and Austrian soldiers arrived we found

that they were worse [than us]. We attributed their behaviour to their contacts with the Turks. And when the British army arrived, we found that they were even more degenerate, for there is no vice and immodesty that is beyond them. We concluded that war is the source of this moral corruption, especially since the city population, and especially those who live in the vicinity of army camps were much more degenerate than those who lived in villages and towns away from military centres.[13]

Yet despite the writers' judgmental tone, they had been ambivalent about the impact of war on Palestine's destiny. They believed that war brought some degree of progress, discipline, and certainly nationalism to the Arab East. Their fears stemmed as much from uncertainty about the new secular modernity as from unease about the unknown future of Palestine after the loss of the Ottoman motherland.

In the annals of World War I much rethinking about the evolution of Arab and Turkish nationalism is under way. Among Arab historians, this has mainly taken the form of rectifying the nationalist historiography of scholars like Khaldun Sati Husari.[14] On the Turkish side, scholars are also a reexamining the idea of an Arab "betrayal" of the Ottomans during the Arab Revolt of 1916–18. Historian Gurcel Goncu noted recently that Arab recruits constituted about three hundred thousand soldiers, a third of the Ottoman forces in 1914—far more than the number of soldiers who followed the banner of the Arab Revolt.[15] In the 2004 ceremonies marking the eighty-eighth anniversary of the Ottoman victory at Gallipoli, the participation of individual soldiers from countries such as New Zealand, Australia, and other Western nations was duly noted, but not the huge [non]presence of soldiers from the Arab provinces, all of whom were subsumed under the Ottoman banner.

Australian historian Bill Sellers noted that Mustafa Kemal (Ataturk) owed his defeat of Allied attacks largely to the fighting stamina of his Arab recruits. "Two-thirds of the troops who made up his 19th Division ... who faced the first wave of the Allied invasion were Syrian Arabs [soldiers from Lebanon, Jordan, Syria, and Palestine], comprising the 72nd and 77th regiments of the Ottoman army."[16] Of the eighty-seven thousand troops who died defending Gallipoli and the Dardanelles Straits, many were Arabs. Yet these victories are portrayed today as Turkish, not Ottoman, victories. This pattern is equally true for the battles of al 'Arish, Suez, Gaza, Megiddo, and Kut al Amara, where native soldiers (Iraqi, Hijazi, Palestinian, and Syrian recruits) were a large component of the Ottoman troops. Below I examine the diaries of three World War I soldiers whose lives were irrevocably transformed by the war: Mehmet (Muhammad) Fasih, of Mersin; Ihsan Turjman, of Jerusalem; and Aref Shehadeh, also of Jerusalem.

WAR DIARIES:
MERSIN, JERUSALEM, AND SIBERIA

Our three soldier-diarists came from distant sides of the Arab provinces of the Ottoman Empire and were unknown to each other, yet the diverse trajectories of their lives, as soldiers in the sultan's army, encapsulate the three major ways in which the Great War transformed the lives of its citizens: through immersion in republican Turkish nationalism (Aref Shehadeh, who was held in a Siberian prison camp for the bulk of the war), a turn to Arab separatism (Second Lieutenant Mehmet Fasih), or a renewed embrace of local urban identity (Private Turjman). In keeping a daily record of their war experiences, the soldiers preserved for posterity a vivid narrative of the great divide that separated the communitarian, multiethnic, imperial domain of the end of the nineteenth century from the nationalist era of the post–World War I period. The three men, by coincidence, were born around 1893, and all were conscripted between July and November 1914—after the declaration of *seferberlik*, the general mobilization that brought Turkey into the war with Germany and the Central powers against the Allied forces.[17] They all came from middle or mercantile classes. Fasih's father was a customs clerk, while the elder Turjman was an old city merchant from a landed family that had lost the bulk of its wealth. The elder Aref was also a shopkeeper from Jerusalem.[18] To find three ordinary soldiers in the imperial army writing daily diaries is remarkable for this period of mass illiteracy. For these diaries to have survived and come to light almost a century after the event is also exceptional, for even among the elite literati, very few ventured to record their observations, and of those, fewer still had their records become available to the public. The narratives of Shehadeh, Fasih, and Turjman are particularly valuable in that they record the impact of the war on their society, document their personal transformations, and describe the trauma the war produced in their officers and comrades.

Unlike Turjman, who spent the war years "playing with my moustache" and using all his skills and family connections to evade being sent to the southern front in Suez, Muhammad Fasih was a decorated soldier who fought courageously in Gallipoli—and later in Gaza and Beersheba. He had little hesitation in sacrificing his life for the sultan and his Ottoman homeland. Significantly, the two men's diaries show that the Great War, at least in its early phases, was able to command considerable loyalty from both its Turkish and Arab citizens for a common future. The contrasting lives of the two soldiers are intriguing in that they show the complex ethnic identities that colored their lives. Turjman came from an Arabized family, possibly of Turkish descent, which settled in Palestine, while the ethnic identity of Fasih is more difficult to discern. According to Murat Çulcu, his father came from a clan that originally settled in the Erguban country of Malayta and later migrated to Mersin, a mixed city of Arabs and Turks in the Syrian province of Iskenderun. His mother, Şefika Hanım, was from the Gedikoğlu family.[19] Ottoman historian Irvin Schick believes, based on Fasih's family's names, that he was Kurdish, or at least half-Kurdish.[20] But the linguistically mixed environment of Mersin when Fasih grew up, and the substantive use of Arabic vocabulary in his diary, indicate that he was familiar with Arabic. And even though he wrote in Ottoman Turkish, his text is full of Arabic usages, which gave considerable difficulty to his Turkish editor.[21] In the one episode of his diaries when he wanted to cheer his comrades trapped in the trenches of Gallipoli, he and a fellow Mersini soldier, Agati, sing Damascene songs in Arabic.[22] Most likely (given his name), Fasih's father was an Arab and his mother was a Turk, since he moved to Istanbul with her when his father died. In 1934 Fasih was compelled to Turkify his name into Mehmet Kayabali to comply with the new republican regulation that required citizens to adopt Turkish last names.[23] In any case, the ambivalence of Fasih's ethnic background and of Turjman's Jerusalem identity are markers of inclusive Ottoman affinities in which the borders of Arab and Turkish ethnicities were not clearly defined.

Fasih and Turjman, although both in their early twenties, could not have been further apart in character. Fasih was highly disciplined and completely devoted to the Ottoman war effort. He had internalized the ranking system of the army and saw himself as a career soldier whose ambition was to move ahead in the hierarchy. For his devotion he was decorated and promoted, ultimately reaching the rank of brigadier general. To him, martyrdom in combat was both acceptable and necessary, but also traumatizing. His eulogy for his friend Nuri is the most moving passage in his diary:

> [Friday, November 5, 1915]
>
> I bury Nuri. It was God's will that I would be the one to bury his remains. Who knows who else I will be burying? After the last shovel of earth, I conduct the religious rites. As I recite al Fatiha, with all the compassion, conviction and eloquence I can muster, I again find it most difficult to control myself. Warm tears stream down my cheeks. As everything must, this also ends. . . . But then another voice insists that neither Nuri, nor all those who preceded him are truly dead, never to see again. It says, "They are temporarily dead. They will come back to life." In that olive grove lie Shakeeb, Izzat, Rashad, Munib (Şekib, İzzet, Reşad, Münib) and many other comrades.[24]

Four days later, on November 9, Fasih told his battalion commander that he was prepared to become the regiment's *feda'i* to carry a sacrificial commando operation.[25] His commander restrained his zeal.

Martyrdom, by contrast, was the last thing on Ihsan's mind. His main objective was to survive the war in order to marry his sweetheart, Thurayya. Turjman was easygoing and nonchalant, and he served in the army out of compulsion. He continuously questioned the political objectives of the war and celebrated the defeat of his own leaders and their German allies. Nevertheless, both he and Fasih found solace in the camaraderie of the army and were distressed when members of their battalions (or in the case of Turjman, his fellow soldiers) were injured or killed.

Their social life was mainly defined by the lives of their comrades and officers.

Shehadeh, in contrast, found his vocation in a journalism career, which he pursued in Istanbul while still a student. Having an eye on a career in the civil service—which he began as a trainee in the foreign ministry—he entered an experimental period before the war that defined what his relationship would be to the governing authority in Jordan and Palestine after the war. Neither Fasih's religiosity nor his acceptance of army discipline prevented him from criticizing the brutality inflicted by officers on subordinates. In one diary entry he expressed his rage at an officer who was whipping a sick soldier to move on:

> This incident, and many others of the kind, demonstrates that, from the lowest to the highest, many are those who fail to appreciate the true value of our ordinary soldier. He is the backbone of the army. He is the one who does all the work. No army can do without him. Regardless of what officer you put at his head, be he German or otherwise, regardless of whether his uniform is khaki or grey, one must know how to deal with his soul, his spirit.[26]

But such moments of reflection are exceptional in Fasih's writing. The thrust of his diary was to keep a record of military operations and his role in them. His writing is precise, matter of fact, and telegraphic in style. Turjman, by contrast, is mainly reflective, discursive, and meandering. He appears to seek in his diary an intimate outlet for his forbidden private thoughts, political and personal. Since Fasih's essay has already been published in Turkish and English, and Shehadeh's diary is still not available in complete form, I focus here on Turjman's manuscript, using the Shehadeh and Fasih diaries, as well as the published memoirs of Cemal Pasha's private secretary, Lieutenant Falih Rıfkı, to provide the necessary historical context.

CHRONICLE OF A DISAPPEARANCE

Ihsan's diary was one of the first casualties of war. It disappeared after his sudden death, just before the end of the war, only to surface almost a century later in a most unusual place. Apparently his parents and his siblings were not aware of its existence, so they did not notice its absence. He must have hidden it for safekeeping with an acquaintance, possibly with Hasan Khalidi, his cousin and closest confidant. During the mid-1920s, the Turjmans, like many middle-class Jerusalemites during the Mandate years, moved out of the old city to a new house in the Musrara neighborhood, near Prophets Street. The area became known as *hayy al Turjman,* because the family had inherited a substantial piece of land in that area (alluded to in the diary, when Ihsan notes that the municipality sequestered part of the family's property to build a connecting road). The family sold one *dunum* (one thousand square meters, or approximately a quarter acre) of the property to architect Andoni Baramki, who built a two-story family dwelling on it. During the war of 1948 the area came under heavy bombardment since it was at the seam of the fighting between the Haganah and the Arab Legion. After the armistice the area was deserted and became a no-man's-land. For two decades the Mandelbaum Gate, in *hayy al Turjman,* was the only entry point connecting the Jewish part of the city to the Arab one, under U.N. supervision. When Israel occupied the eastern part of the city in 1967, it annexed the whole area to the western part of the city and eventually—in 1999— built the Turjman House: Museum of the Seam in the bullet-ridden Baramki building. The building was renamed the Turjman Post, an oblique allusion to its original owners, and both the Baramkis and the Turjmans attempted for many years, in vain, to reclaim their confiscated property through Israeli courts.[27] The diary itself, lost since 1917, resurfaced in the 1970s in the Abandoned Arab Property section of the Hebrew University library.[28] When the diary was first discovered, its author was unknown. The handwritten name on the diary, "Muhammad Salih," was a false lead and did not indicate the true name of the author. The only published reference to this diary appeared in Adel Manaʻ's *History of Palestine at the Ottoman Era (1700–1918)*, published in 1999.[29] In discussing Cemal Pasha's campaign against deserting soldiers during World War I, he refers to a diary by a Jerusalem soldier named Muhammad Adil Salih who was stationed in Jerusalem and who narrated "the suffering of soldiers during the war." Another scholar who used the manuscript, Abigail Jacobson, also refers to the author as Muhammad Salih.[30] A 1949 catalogue in the National Library contains a list of West Jerusalem Arab households from which property and papers were appropriated by the Haganah. The following line appeared in the list: Adel Hassan Turjmans—St. Paul St.[31] St. Paul was the street in Musrara to which the Turjmans moved in the early 1920s from the old city, and Adel was the youngest of Hasan Bey's sons. Thus, the National Library became the silent depository of Ihsan's war diary by virtue of military conquest.

Why the manuscript was listed under the name of Muhammad Adel Salih is not clear. Salih was the legal name of the Turjmans, and Adel was Hasan Bey's son and Ihsan's youngest brother, so it is possible that the papers were taken from the family house in 1948. When I acquired a photocopy of the diary in 2005, the family was not aware of its existence. Moreover, nothing on the cover indicates the real name of the author. The only direct clue to his identity was the appearance of the name Ihsan five or six times in passages in which family members address the writer. Luckily I found another diary, that of Khalil Sakakini, Ihsan's teacher and friend, then also unpublished, which included entries for 1915 and 1916. I was able to trace four instances in which entries in the two diaries corresponded. Of these four entries *only one*—for Sunday, March 31, 1915—recorded a visit by Turjman to Sakakini. In it the diarist discusses a visit to his former teacher in which the subject of Sakakini's impending conscription dominated the evening. The writer offers to have his family intervene with the mayor to help him pay the exemption fee *(badal)* of 50 Ottoman pounds in lieu of military service.[32] Sakakini's March 31 entry makes the following observation: "I must register here my gratitude to my friend Hussein Effendi Salim Husseini, the mayor, for he offered to pay 22 Ottoman liras to pay half of my *badal*. I was also told that his niece, the daughter of Zaki Dawoodi offered to arrange for the *badal* in conversation with my sister Milia. Ihsan Turjman informed me that his family are very worried about me, considering me one of their members, when they heard that I am to be sent as a soldier to Beisan."[33] With this entry the name of the author was finally revealed.

An enigmatic feature of Ihsan's diary is the use of a cryptogram, which he called *shifra,* a secret numerical code in accordance with Ottoman military encryption practices, to express his inner thoughts. This occurs in two sections of the diary. The first one deals with his relationship to Thurayya, his woman friend, where the purpose was obviously to protect her identity and to hide his longing for her. In the second section the purpose of the coded entries is less clear. Initially the reader might think that he sought to hide his association with opposition groups within the army, but this explanation does not make sense given the ferocity of his attacks on Cemal and Enver Pashas in plain language. Upon closer examination we discover an association between the coded messages and references to his dispute with his father. The frequency of their occurrence increases when Ihsan recounts the scandalous theft of the family jewelry during the Turjmans' temporary move outside the city walls in the autumn of 1916. The culprits were caught when they tried to sell the jewelry (mostly belonging to his two aunts), and they turned out to be his cousins from the Abul Su'ud family. The incident was particularly traumatic for Ihsan since he had to give testimony against his cousins to the police interrogator, and then again in a public court hearing. He tried unsuccessfully to persuade his father to drop the case, but his father persisted. At this point, Ihsan began to use the numerically coded messages to discuss his controversy with his father. The use of cryptogams here is fascinating since an educated person like Turjman had the option of using another literary code known as *hisab al jummal*, often used by poets to convert secret words into numbers, but he decided to create his own numerical system to provide added caution against discovery, given that the literary code was probably easy to breach. The writer kept a coded key to his cryptogram, which he deposited with his cousin for safekeeping.

IN THE SERVICE OF RUŞEN BEY

Ihsan Salih Turjman, who grew up in the old city, was conscripted into the Ottoman army in November 1914, when he was twenty-three years old. He was first stationed in Dhahriyyeh in the Hebron district and then moved to Nablus, before drawing on his family's connections to acquire a post in the Jerusalem central military command, where he could commute to work from his home near Bab al Silsilah, inside the Haram (al Aqsa Mosque) area. Early in 1915 he began to keep a daily diary

Figure 2. Ihsan Turjman, private, in
Ottoman army uniform, Jerusalem,
1915. Courtesy Turjman family.

of his intimate thoughts and activities as a way of venting his
frustration at the drudgery of military life.[34] In doing so he was
emulating his teacher and mentor Khalil Effendi Sakakini at al-
Dusturiyya College, who had been keeping a diary since 1906
and often read excerpts to his inner circle.

The Turjmans, officially known as the Salih family in court
records, were an established clerical family who served for several centuries in the Ottoman civil service and in the Islamic
court of Jerusalem as translators—hence their name.[35] One of
Ihsan's great-grandfathers was Qasim Bey Turjman, in whose
name a *sabeel* (public water fountain) was endowed near al
Haram area (opposite Bab al Silsilah) in 1701. He owned an open
court market in Bab al Amud and acquired substantial properties in the old city.[36] Another ancestor, Ahmad Bey Turjman,
lived in Haret al Sharaf, near what became the Jewish Quarter,
and owned a large plaza in the area known as Sahit Ahmad Bey
Turjman.[37] Both were prominent translators in the court.

Ihsan's father, Hasan Bey Salih, inherited much of this property, but most of it was tied up in public endowments, or leased land. The family lived inside the Haram at the entrance of Bab al Silsilah in a three-story house that overlooked the Haram plaza from the east and the Wailing Wall and the Magharbeh Quarter from the south. Hasan Bey lived for two decades in a childless marriage until his first wife prevailed on him (according to contemporary stories) to marry his second wife, Nabiha Khalili—descended from Sheikh Ali Khalili, a prominent Jerusalemite and one of the first city dwellers to build a mansion outside the city walls in al Baq'a neighborhood. Nabiha bore him six children (three boys and three girls), of whom Ihsan was the eldest.[38] But Hasan remained faithful to his first wife, Safiyyah, and continued to live with her after his second marriage, in a separate apartment in the third floor of their home, until she died during the first war.

Ihsan grew up with Safiyyah as his second mother. He studied in Qur'anic schools by the Haram and then went to a local *nizamiyyeh* school for his primary education. After 1909 he joined Khalil Sakakini's Dusturiyya College, which offered an Arab secular curriculum. To the end of his life Ihsan considered Sakakini his mentor and confidant, as is evident from his diary.

When the general mobilization was announced by the Ottoman government in November 1914, Ihsan was conscripted and sent to central Palestine. Just before he was to be sent to the Suez front in Sinai, he was transferred to Jerusalem's military headquarter to serve under the commander Ali Ruşen Bey.

Ruşen Bey was an Albanian officer whose administrative skills earned him a promotion to *qa'immaqam* (deputy governor), which put him in charge of army logistics in the southern front. His headquarters, the Commissariat, were in the sequestered

Notre Dame building opposite Jerusalem's New Gate.[39] In this position he became the highest military officer in Ottoman Palestine, subject only to Cemal Pasha, commander of the Fourth Army. The latter was based in Damascus during the war and visited Jerusalem periodically.

Ali Ruşen's official title was residence inspector *(mufattish manzil)*, and his domain included the mobilization and training of soldiers for military and auxiliary tasks and the overall administration of army logistics—feeding, munitions, and the setting up of army camps in southern Palestine.[40] Omar Salih attributes the initial success of the Ottomans on the Egyptian front to the organizational skills of Ruşen Bey.[41] Ali Ruşen remained in Jerusalem to the very end of the war, where he commanded a battalion and fought tenaciously—according to an eyewitness account—against Allenby's advancing army in Nebi Samuel.[42] He was last seen leading his battalion in retreat to the village of Gib. Aside from local contemporary sources, such as the Barghouti and Jawhariyyeh memoirs, very few records provide information about the fate of Ali Ruşen Bey. Ottoman military archives contain four telegrams sent in code from the governor of Sivas, Muhyi ed-Din, that mention Ruşen Bey in reports of military maneuvers involving Mustafa Kemal, all dated Huzeiran 1335 (June 1919), so he must have still been active in Anatolia toward the end of the war.[43]

Ihsan served as a petty clerk in Ruşen's headquarters. His main tasks, aside from "when I was just sitting there playing with my moustache," were to review petitions for exemption from service and to file paperwork within the Ottoman military bureaucracy. In that capacity he was privy to political discussions among Turkish, Albanian, and Syrian officers in Palestine—as well as the occasional German visiting officers—and could observe the deteriorating mood of the rank and file. His diary, written daily by candlelight during the early war years, reflects the cosmology of a common soldier and a plebian citizen of the city at a critical period of Palestine's history, when of four centuries of Ottoman rule were ending and an unknown future lay ahead, as the British army advanced on Gaza and Beersheba from the south and bombarded Jaffa and Haifa from the sea.

Almost every chronicle that we have inherited from the period was authored by a political leader (Awni Abdul Hadi, Muhammad Izzat Darwazeh, and Rustum Haydar), a military commander (Fawzi Quwakgi), or an intellectual-activist (Sakakini, Najati Sidqi). Ihsan's diary is unique in providing the detailed observations of a foot soldier, written with intimacy and simple but keen reflections on an encircled city. As such it is one of the few surviving subaltern chronicles of the Ottoman period. Because Ihsan commuted daily to work from his family house in the old city, he lived in two worlds—the military circles of the Ottoman officer corps and the tribulations of the urban street in times of war. His diary contains a wealth of observation on daily life in Jerusalem in 1915 and 1916, the reactions of the urban poor and artisans to deprivation, and the disasters that accompanied the locust attacks and the army confiscation of property, means of transport, and work animals. But the diary is also full of intimate social details about the soldier's private life: his love affair with a neighboring woman, his daily visits to his teacher and mentor, his disgust at the debaucheries of his commanding officers, his constant (and failed) attempts to evade army service, the role of rumors in the life of the city, his detective work to uncover the identity of the thief that robbed his house and his shame at finding out that his cousins were responsible, his rift with his father and family on this subject, and the devastation caused by cholera, famine, locust attacks, and the wholesale forced movement of populations. Ihsan survived all of these disasters only to be fatally shot by an Ottoman officer of the withdrawing Ottoman army in 1917. He never saw his twenty-fifth birthday.[44]

Ihsan's world was permeated by war and by the impending catastrophe: his disrupted studies, scenes of disease and hunger in the streets, the absence of tobacco and other goods from stores, and his declining prospects for marriage to his beloved as his fortunes and his family income began to dissipate. Ihsan's despair seems to echo William Pfaff's belief that "the moral function of war [has been] to recall humans to the reality at the core of existence: the violence that is part of our nature and is responsible for the fact that human history is a chronicle of tragedies."[45]

THE DECENTERING OF PALESTINE: THE EGYPTIAN OPTION

The Turjman diary opens with a self-interrogation about the destiny of the Holy Land after the war. "We more or less agreed that the days of the [Ottoman] state are numbered, and that its dismemberment is imminent. But what will be the fate of Palestine?" When he wrote this entry on March 28, 1915, the fate of the empire was the burning issue of debate among his fellow soldiers, his officers, his family, and the members of his social circle whom he met daily in the municipal park and in the cafés inside Jaffa Gate.

His answer reflects the mood of the street at that moment, but it is one that runs contrary to conventional wisdom about the popular currents prevailing in Palestine at the turn of the century. Not Syria—*bilad al Sham*—was the destiny for Palestine, but Egypt.

We all saw two possibilities: independence or annexation to Egypt. The last possibility is more likely since only the English are likely to possess this country, and England is unlikely to give full sovereignty to Palestine but is more liable to annex it to Egypt and create a single dominion ruled by the khedive of Egypt. Egypt is our neighbor, and since both countries contain a majority of Muslims, it makes sense to annex it and crown the viceroy of Egypt as king of Palestine and the Hijaz.[46]

What is striking about this observation is not its contemplation of the possibility of Palestine's independence in the post-Ottoman settlement, but the fact that it does not reflect, even as an alternative, the presumed consensus of the nationalist movement in that period—that Palestine would be annexed as the southern Syrian province in an autonomous Arab East. This perceived merger (or annexation) when the Hashemite leadership was on the eve of announcing the Arab Revolt of 1916 and negotiating an alliance with the Syrian nationalist forces in Damascus.

There is no doubt, however, that the pro-Syrian wing in the Arabist movement in Palestine was quite strong and was represented in the Ottoman Decentralization Party (which wanted autonomy for the Arab region within a reformulated arrangement with Istanbul) as well as in secret secessionist groups such as al Arabiyya al Fatah and al 'ahd group. In central Palestine these tendencies were articulated by political activists like Muhammad Izzat Darwazeh and Awni Abdul Hadi, the future leaders of al Istiqlal Party, which considered Palestine the southern region of an independent Syria.

Turjman's comments suggest an amorphous political atmosphere that opened up several future possibilities for Palestine (and Syria) during World War I. In noting the desire for a merger with Egypt, Turjman was not uttering an isolated political

Figure 3. Palestinian leaders representing various factions after the war, including Awni Abdul Hadi, Haj Amin Husseini, Musa Kazim Pasha Husseini, and Ragheb bey Nashashibi, later mayor of Jerusalem, c. 1926. Institute for Palestine Studies, Beirut.

thought. He was reflecting a position that was heatedly debated (although by no means adopted) among soldiers in Jerusalem's central command and among his inner circle of friends. Quite a few intellectuals during the war harbored hopes for the retention of Palestine within a reconstructed (and constitutional) Ottoman regime. Some of these proponents were outright Ottomans and close allies of Cemal Pasha's political line. Most notable among these well-known political figures were Sheikh As'ad Shuqairi from Akka, Mufti Taher Abul Su'ud and Ali Rimawi from Jerusalem, and Sheikh Salim Ya'coubi from Jaffa. Darwazeh describes how the Committee of Union and Progress (CUP) mobilized them in September 1915 to go on a publicity tour to Istanbul and Gallipoli, under the guise of supporting the war effort, where they openly attacked the Arab nationalists for "undermining the unity of the Sultanate and Turkish Arab brotherhood."[47] CUP, whose members were commonly known as the Young Turks, was a movement formed at the turn of the nineteenth century by various ethnic groups in the Ottoman Empire in opposition to the oppressive regime of Sultan Abdülhamid II. It became a political party in 1906 and came to power in 1908. The group included a number of pro-Ottoman journalists, including Muhammad Kurd Ali, owner of the widely circulating Damascene newspaper *al-Muqtabis,* to create an atmosphere favorable to the repression of the secessionist movement. In Gallipoli, according to Mehmet Fasih, the group was welcomed by Turkish and Arab fighters alike. On October 21, 1915, Fasih wrote, "17:30 hrs ... delegation of Syrian literati visits Regimental HQ with a gift of Damascus *baklava* for the officers. Each of us receives a slice."[48] According to Darwazeh, however, Cemal Pasha used the support of this group to justify his repression of the Arab nationalist movement, including the hanging of its leaders in Beirut.[49]

Most Ottoman loyalists in this period, however, were not hostile to Arab nationalism. They included a number of people who until recently had had sympathies with the CUP or with the Ottoman Decentralization Party, such as Omar Salih Barghouti, Is'af Nashashibi, and Khalil Sakakini—all closely associated with Turjman. In this intellectual circle only Adel Jaber, a prominent young lawyer and journalist, continued to identify strongly with the Ottomans for the duration of the war.[50]

A similar debate on the future of Palestine was taking place in the major urban centers of the country. Najib Nassar, editor of *al-Karmil* in Haifa (established in 1908) published a war memoir, *Miflih al Ghassani* (his *nom de plume*), while hiding from Ottoman police, which contains a revealing encounter between Arab officers in the Ottoman army and local nationalists about the situation in the North.[51] Nassar/Miflih reports that with few exceptions, like Sheikh As'ad Shuqairi of Akka and Prince Shakib Arsalan, from Mount Lebanon, the majority of his companions, both inside and outside the army, are strong advocates of Arab nationalist autonomy, and pro-Ottoman unity. Nassar/Miflih believes and fights for Arab-Turkish amity and reconciliation, seeing this step as essential for the stability of the Ottoman regime. Like many young Arab officers in their circle, Nassar/Miflih and his peers struggle to keep the country out of the war, which they believe would be a disaster for Syria and Palestine. In their view, their enemies are the Germans (who want to divert the Allies to Egypt (Suez) away from the western front); the CUP, which has taken an anti-Arab path under Enver and Cemal's leadership; and Zionism, which under the cover of war, is displacing the country's native population with Eastern European immigrants.

These young officers' debate, in contrast to that in Jerusalem circles, is more sophisticated and more directed at Ottoman policy at the local level. Surprisingly they considered one of the main allies of the Arab dissidents in the early period of the war to be Küçük Cemal Pasha (Mersini), based in Damascus as leader of the Eighth Army, whom Miflih described as "judicious, level-headed, friendly to the Arab nationalists, and largely unaffected by the anti-Arab campaign of Ahmad Cemal."[52] At one point, Cemal interceded to lift Nassar's name from the blacklist.[53] In Nassar's dialogue with Sabih, the young Ottoman officer, the latter argued, "We should have an armed neutrality *(hiyad musallah)*, so that by the end of the war, when all the allies are exhausted we [the Ottomans] can annul the Capitulations, and ensure our real independence, before the Allies regain their strength."[54] Miflih/Nassar responded that real independence depended on ending anti-Arab Turkish attitudes and on full equality in citizenship: "Only thus can the Ottoman state be strong enough to stand against colonial schemes. A main obstacle to this independence is the Arab hypocrites [whom he calls "Turkified Arabs"] who kowtow to the Turkish rulers and don't tell them the truth."[55] The seeming paradox is the expression of strong Arab nationalist sentiments in conjunction with an insistence, before and during the war, on the integrity and unity of the Ottoman state. Nassar does not mention the possibility of Arab independence (Syrian or Palestinian) from Istanbul or talk about unity with Egypt. He mentions the latter only in reference to German schemes encouraging Arab nationalists to overthrow the pro-British government there.[56]

In Jerusalem, however, the Egyptian option was very much alive. Like several intellectuals in his company, Ihsan, in his diary, makes his claims for a merger with Egypt on two counts: Palestine is too small to be independent, and British interests would not allow it. This sentiment also reflects his recognition of the underlying aims of the Ottoman campaign in the southern front—to instigate a pro-Ottoman popular rebellion in Egypt against the British administration. Agents of Cemal Pasha, commander of the Fourth Army and governor of Syria, were at work in Cairo, Alexandria, and the Suez region instigating the Egyptian street against the British.[57] The overall objective of the campaign was to disrupt the shipping traffic at the canal and to divert Allied troops from the Dardanelles.[58] Cemal Pasha had in fact organized Arab and Bulgarian Muslim units in a separate battalion named the Islamic Salvation Army of Egypt (Halaskâr Mısır Ordu-yı İslâmiyesi), including Druze units under the leadership of Shakib Arsalan.[59] In his memoirs, published immediately after the war, the CUP leader makes his intentions explicit:

[During the initial attack on Suez] the Arab fighters, who constituted the bulk of the 25th Battalion performed splendidly, which
hardly mitigated my disgust at Sherif Hussein's attempts to plant
the seeds of dissension in this united mass of solidarity [between
Arabs and Turks]. . . . Every time I heard the lyrics of "The Red
Banner Shall Fly over Cairo" which echoed the footsteps of the
throngs leading their way in the darkness of the desert, my heart
became certain of our victory . . . I invested a great deal of hope in
this moment on the support of patriotic Egyptians, whom I had
anticipated would revolt as one man encouraged by the [antici-
pated] fall of Isma'iliyya in the hands of the Ottoman army.[60]

Elsewhere in his memoirs, however, he suggests that the thrust
of the Suez campaign was demonstrative and diversionary: "I
never seriously imagined that we would cross and seize the
Canal, but so thoroughly did I convince HQ and the main units
under my command, no one had any notion that this was a demonstration and no one held back for a moment from displaying
the utmost self-sacrifice."[61] But this comment can also be taken
as a retrospective apologia for his lack of military achievements
in the campaign.

The failure of the Suez campaign—in large part due to bad
Turkish intelligence about the strength of pro-Ottoman forces
in Egypt, underestimation of the fighting capacities of Indian
troops under British command, and Arab troops' weak performance in Sinai—unleashed Cemal Pasha's campaign of repression against the Arab nationalist movement in the spring of 1915.[62]

Turjman's Egypt-centrism was also rooted in the decentering
of Palestine's geography in that period. The boundaries of Ottoman Palestine were delineated by the Mutasarrıflık of Jerusalem, a relatively recent entity (from 1873) that was administered
directly from Istanbul. These boundaries included Jaffa and Sinjil
at the northern frontiers and the great expanses of the Sinai des-

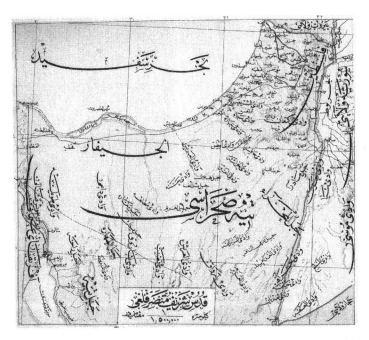

Figure 4. Ottoman Palestine as defined by the boundaries of the Mutasarrıflık of al Quds Al Sharif, 1917. Reprinted from R. Tekin and Y Bas, *Osmanli Atlasi* (Istanbul: Ekim, 2001). Courtesy Institute for Jerusalem Studies.

ert to the south.[63] Although the recognized boundaries between Egypt and Ottoman Palestine were north of al 'Arish, the 1917 Ottoman map of Palestine indicated a Governorship of Jerusalem that extended as far as Port Said and the Suez Canal, with the wilderness of Sahra' al Tayh in Sinai constituting the central focus of the region.[64] Contributing to this decentering of Palestine was the assumption in the cartography of the period that the Suez Canal marked the separation of Ottoman Africa (Afrika-yı Osmanî) from Ottoman Asia (Asya-yı Osmanî). The maps presented the Sinai Peninsula as a natural, if not administrative, extension of the Mutasarrıflık of Kudüs-i Şerîf (Jerusalem).[65]

With the improvement of transportation routes at the turn of the century and with commercial and cultural exchanges between Egypt and Palestine, the Egyptian press became a primary influence on the Jerusalem and Jaffa intelligentsia—much more so than the Beirut or Damascus press. Within Jerusalem intellectual circles, Is'af Nashashibi was particularly known for his Egyptian cultural affinities. He later wrote a polemical essay on the Arabness of Egypt in which he attacked those who favored the separation of Egypt from its Arab environment: "Those who question the Arabness of Egypt and the Egyptian roots of Arabness, are a retrograde burning with anti-Islamic hatred, and poisoned by Western propaganda."[66] Sakakini wrote primarily for the Cairene *al Masa'* and *al Muqattam* in this period, and Ihsan's diary shows that he was a regular reader of *al Hilal,* and *al Muqtatif* when they arrived in Jerusalem. With the exception of *al Himara al Qahira* (The Stubborn Donkey) and *Filasteen*—which was suspended in Jaffa most of the war years—all of his reading material came from Cairo.

The possibility of creating an Egyptian-Palestinian condominium, and sometimes an Egyptian-Syrian federation, was at one point widely discussed within Arabist circles, including among those still active in Ottoman political parties, even before the Great War. Salim Salam, a Beirut member of the Ottoman parliament and an important advocate of decentralization, describes in his memoirs a meeting with Khedive Abbas Hilmi Pasha as early as February 1912 in which the two men discussed the possibility of a Syrian-Egyptian union. He was sent on a mission to intercede with the Egyptian authorities on behalf of the Ottomans to allow armed groups fighting against the Italian occupation forces in Libya to gain safe passage through Egyptian territories.[67] He mentions that as a result of the Ottoman defeat in the Balkan War, Syrian nationalists sought to join Egypt under British protection.[68] Wajih Kawtharani, the Lebanese historian, quotes a secret report by the French consul in Beirut that confirms that Deputy Salam was sent to Egypt, under the guise of soliciting aid from Libyan rebels, to negotiate Syrian unity with Egypt and indicates that the khedive received him with that purpose in mind.[69]

Within three years, however, this mood shifted noticeably. Ottoman retreat and British control of Palestine made the idea of merging with Egypt far-fetched, and the independence of Palestine created fears within the nationalist currents that it would have to face the Zionist movement alone. Palestinians went back to favoring a greater Syria. "The idea of joining Palestine to Syria is spreading powerfully those days," wrote Khalil Sakakini in his diary on January 20, 1919: "People say: Palestine and Syria are two sisters visited together by catastrophes so far, and by a common thirst for freedom and independence. Now they must have the same fate, and under no circumstance should one be amputated from the other. At the same time the notion of 'Palestine for the Palestinians' and full independence is retreating, and you have many people who are against the idea [of independence] altogether."[70]

LIVING IN THREE TIME ZONES: OTTOMAN/GREGORIAN/HIJRI

The modernity of Ottoman Palestine created a disjointed universe that was most visible in the divided time zones as people made daily transitions from the domestic unit to the public sphere. Army regulations introduced new notions of timekeeping aimed at regimenting soldiers' cycle of work and ensuring discipline. Mehmet Fasih's diary entries while he was in Gallipoli itemized his daily chores by the minute. Here is a typical entry, for November 26, 1915:

> 22.30 hrs Go to bed. Impossible to sleep. New orders keep pouring in. 57th, 27th, and 25th regiments are to carry out reconnaissance probes.
>
> 01.30 hours Written order arrives. Get up. Division orders us to prepare a reconnaissance patrol to be commanded by an officer . . .
>
> 02.00 hrs Prepare my report. No incidents. Are awaiting orders. Go back to bed.
>
> 03.09 hrs Get up. No orders yet. Men are ready. Officers from Engineers drop in . . . plans abandoned.[71]

No such minutiae exist for Turjman, but he does record his activities in fractions of the hour ("lunch 12:20, meeting with Taher Effendi, 4:40; went to bed 11:45"). These categories of time segments were—for Palestine—a novelty that began to gain dominance in World War I. Soldiers internalized them and began to alter the ways in which they marked their tempo in the civilian sphere. In Europe, as well as in Istanbul and Egypt, tower clocks had been introduced to public buildings and public squares in the nineteenth century, but in greater Syria and Palestine, the new methods of keeping time were more recent, the most notable example being the Jaffa Gate clock tower celebrating the anniversary of Sultan Abdülhamid's assumption to the throne (in 1901), which extended army discipline and government departments to the public at large. Gelvin suggests that the Jerusalem public clock represented the intersection between "time and work discipline," exemplifying "the attempt to regulate Jerusalem's labour force and make it submissive to a daily, nine-to-five type of schedule."[72]

Turjman used three calendar notations (Ottoman/Rumi, Gregorian/Western, and Hijri) and two time zones (Arab and *franji*) in his daily diary entries. The Ottoman notations regulated all financial and military matters, such as paydays, military commands, and regulations. The Gregorian calendar regulated political events and major events of the war—such as dates of battles and of the entry of competing armies—as well as Jerusalem's relationship to the external world. The Hijri calendar marked the approaching holidays and ceremonial events. Throughout Palestine, farmers used a fourth calendar, the Julian (Eastern Orthodox) calendar, to mark the cycle of agricultural crops—sowing, harvesting, and preparing for the winter provisions. At the time (and even today in large parts of the rural Middle East), Christians and Muslims alike widely believed that the Julian calendar is more attuned to nature's cycles than the Hijri, Ottoman, or Western calendars. Some city folks, such as Sakakini, used the Julian calendar in their daily lives to mark major events, including the coming of the new year. Ihsan's world was also regulated by two timing systems. The *franji* system marked working hours in military headquarters and determined rendezvous times with friends and acquaintances. Those times were kept through pocket watches, which were expensive but within the means of ordinary citizens. We know that Ihsan had a pocket watch because he describes an episode in which he kept taking his watch apart until "my idiotic mind ruined the spring mechanism."

Arabic time divided the day into five spans punctuated by prayer times and regulated fasting periods as well as the end of the working day at sunset. "Arab time" divided the day into twelve hours of sunlight beginning with sunrise and ending in sunset.[73] Some clocks, such as the sundial in the Haram area near the Turjman house, bridged the two timekeeping systems, and Ihsan moved relatively smoothly from one system to another ("I met him at 4 P.M. *franji,* equivalent to ten o'clock Arabic time," is an example of the type of double notation he commonly used), just as he worked simultaneously with the three daily calendars. All entries were duly made in Ottoman, Gregorian, and Hijri notations. Occasionally, however, confusion reigns in his entries, such as when he visits his neighbors during the Asha'—and it is not clear whether he is having his supper with them or joining them for evening prayer.

As with the army of Muhammad Ali Pasha a century earlier, army discipline at Notre Dame's military headquarters inculcated in the young Palestinian conscripts notions of discipline and time awareness that transformed their daily habits. Work shifts, lunch breaks, afternoon breaks, evening shifts, and so on were keenly observed. The military Commissariat at Notre Dame was the first building in Jerusalem to introduce electric power (1915) through its own generators, which created the possibility of a twenty-four-hour working day. In Ihsan's mind the Commissariat represented modernity, exemplified by army uniforms, electric lighting, and the automobile, while his home near the Haram, where he wrote his memoirs late at night by candlelight, represented tradition.

UNSENTIMENTAL EDUCATION

Ihsan's world outlook was at once secular, pacifist, and compassionate. One is struck by his cosmopolitan outlook given his traditional family milieu, limited education, and even more limited life experience and young age when he was drafted into the army. We know that his father, Hasan, had insisted that his sons and daughters receive a Qur'anic education before they went on (mostly) to secular schools.[74] His natural (i.e., nonideological) pacifism was no doubt a reaction to the carnage of the war and the high death rate from disease and famine during World War I. But his outlook was formed basically through his interaction with several intellectual figures: Omar Salih al Barghouti, Adel Jaber, Musa Alami, Khalil Sakakini, Is'af Nashashibi, and his cousin Hasan Khalidi, who had just received his medical degree from Beirut. Within this group Ihsan, still a young and impressionable soldier, was mainly an observer. To these we must add the towering figure of Rustum Haydar, the deputy director of al-Salahiyya College in Damascus, who visited Jerusalem frequently and who met with Turjman during one of his visits to the home of Sakakini, his teacher at al-Dusturiyya College (established in 1909). Ihsan visited his teacher/mentor at least three or four times a week during the war years, and it was here that he met Haydar. Sakakini gave him the idea of recording his thoughts in a diary, but more significantly, Ihsan absorbed his teacher's critical thinking about nationalism and his progressive views on children's education and the emancipation of women.

The diversity of Turjman's close circle of friends challenges the prevailing assumption that the only place Arabs could acquire a secular and modernist education in the late Ottoman period was the mission schools (such as the Russian seminaries in Nazareth and Beit Jala, the La Salles Brothers in Jaffa and Jerusalem, St Joseph's Schools and the Sisters of Zion, and Bishop Gobat's schools). Sakakini, aided by advocates of the Arab Enlightenment such as Nakhleh Zureik, succeeded in establishing an educational system that challenged the confessional system and attracted hundreds of students from Palestine who chose to avoid the sectarianism of the Christian missionaries.

Al-Dusturiyya College (later known as al-Wataniyya College) was established in 1909 in the spirit of the new Ottoman constitution, basically as a protest against the (Greek) ecclesiastical orthodox hierarchy. Here Ihsan received his basic education, and he continued to associate with al-Dusturiyya graduates and teachers while in the military.

For the military elite, the Imperial War Academy in Istanbul and the regional military colleges in cities like Damascus and Baghdad introduced a select few students to a "national" alternative to the missionary schools. But another, often-overlooked intellectual current was the modernist Ottoman educational system introduced after the revolution of 1908. Most public schools in Jerusalem began to introduce secular curricula along European lines. The most important public school in the city was al Rashidiyya, which graduated leading figures of reform in that period. Reformers such as Sheikh Muhammad Salih were inspired by the Islamic reformism of Jamal Din Afghani and Muhammad Abdo. Sheikh Salih established al Rawda al Faiha', which took the daring step of converting all history, geography, literature, and religious texts from Turkish to Arabic.[75]

The most important Ottoman college in Palestine in Ihsan's day was al-Salahiyya, established in 1913 at Cemal Pasha's initiative on the grounds of St. Anne's (a crusader church near the Haram area that was confiscated from the French during the war). Selâhaddîn-i Eyyûbî Kulliye-i İslâmiyesi, as it was known in Turkish, was Cemal's ambitious attempt to train a generation of pro-Ottoman Arab intelligentsia. The college provided twelve years of studies in two phases after primary education and was therefore a university-level institute; its curriculum was a mixture of theological studies and the latest secular disciplines available in that period.[76] The college was administered by three protégés of Cemal Pasha: Abdel Aziz Shawish, Shakib Arsalan, and Abdul Qadir Mughrabi, all of whom were early supporters of the Young Turk movement and champions of Ottoman decentralization. But the most important figure in Salahiyya was Rustum Haydar (1886–1940), who established the secret Arab society al Jamʻiyya al Arabiyya al Fatat (Society of Young Arabs) in 1911 with Awni Abdul Hadi and Ahmad Qadri.[77] Haydar appears prominently in Turjman's diary as a friend of Sakakini and a fierce exponent of Arabism in the Ottoman state. In 1918 he escaped from Damascus with Sakakini to Jabal Druze to join the Arab rebellion under the leadership of Prince Faisal. Two other prominent intellectuals from Turjman's circle of friends were also on the faculty at al-Salahiyya: Isʻaf Nashashibi, who taught Arabic, and Adel Jaber, who taught French and geography. Sakakini also taught at al-Salahiyya, when his busy schedule at his own college allowed him.

In his diary Turjman expressed hostility toward both Nashashibi and Jaber for their arrogance and elitism. But he was particularly venomous toward Adel Jaber, whom he accused of being an apologist for Cemal Pasha and, at one point, a secret agent for the government.[78] In an entry on May 15, 1915, he notes that Jaber was sent to Jaffa on behalf of Ahmad Cemal Pasha, most likely on a recruitment mission for al-Salahiyya College. At the end of the entry, he approvingly quotes his cousin Hasan Khalidi's comment that Adel Jaber was "an Ottoman spy."[79] Jaber himself never disguised his pro-CUP sentiments and defended Ottoman policy in heated debates with Nashashibi, Sakakini, and Musa Alami throughout the war. In his political leanings, he was not alone. This episode reflects the tension building up between the Arab secessionists and the Ottomanists within the Palestinian (and Syrian-Lebanese) intelligentsia. There is no indication that Ihsan's spying accusation against Jaber was based on fact (however, Adel may secretly have been vying for the attention of Thurayya [Surayya], Ihsan's woman friend). Cemal had a hand in creating this schism in the ranks of Arab political groups, for he sought to foster hostility between what he considered "extreme nationalists" and moderate Arab nationalists.[80] He saw al-Salahiyya as the institutional base from which he could build a loyalist Arab civil service for the new regime.[81]

Another major objective for al-Salahiyya was to create an intellectual base for a pan-Islamic movement under Ottoman sponsorship. According to Martin Strohmeier, Cemal Pasha aimed to train "theologians who would be both open-minded and intellectually equipped to deal with a secular and scientific concepts" in the spirit of Muhammad Abdo.[82] The latter was greatly admired by Sakakini's circle—which later became known as the party of Vagabonds—but the group had moved beyond Abdo's objectives of Islamic reform to adopt essentially secular and (in a few cases) antireligious perspectives. With British troops getting close to southern Palestine, Cemal Pasha moved the premises of the college, together with the students and teaching staff, to Damascus. Subsequently al-Salahiyya College failed in its objectives for two reasons: it was unable to recruit students from outside the Syrian-Palestinian areas (that is from India and Indonesia), as Cemal had anticipated; and it was too short-lived to develop an independent school of thought. After the move to Damascus, most of the college's staff, including Sakakini and Rustum Haydar, defected and joined the Arab rebellion.

Ihsan's reading while serving under Ruşen Bey was very eclectic. His family had a substantial library at home from which Is'af Nashashibi and Musa Alami would borrow books. Ihsan also added a few volumes during his apprenticeship at al-Dusturiyya College. In the long waiting hours at his desk, he read Zamachshari's works and other Arab classics, such as the *History of Arab Civilization* by Muhammad Kurd Ali, who was a chief supporter of al-Salahiyya pan-Islamic program. Ihsan read and admired Qasim Amin's book *Tahrir al Mar'a* (The Liberation of Women, Cairo, 1899). But he also was a heavy consumer of romantic novels—the equivalent of today's pulp fiction. He also read "marriage manuals," such as *Selecting Your Wife (Intikhab al zawja), Night of the Wedding (Lailat al urs),* and *Our Sexual Life (Hayatuna al tanasuliyya)*—mostly by European authors. These were most likely local translations of English and French pamphlets, and Ihsan read them surreptitiously at work for fear of being caught by his father. He notes that his military officers—Turkish, Albanian, and Arab (such as Faris Effendi and Ismail Mani)—rebuked him whenever they caught him reading, mostly out of anti-intellectual motivations rather than concern about his lack of work discipline. At least this is what Turjman claimed. He also read the local press with great enthusiasm. His favorite was *al Himara*, a weekly of political satire that made fun of the leadership of the CUP. The fact that Ihsan had access to this publication suggests that Ottoman censorship during the war years was much more lax than many people have assumed.

THE RUPTURE OF OTTOMAN IDENTITY

With Mehmet Fasih came the loss of Ottoman identity, as the postwar struggles in Anatolia eliminated the CUP from positions of power and the Turkish republican leadership assumed power after successfully eliminating the Greek, British, and other European armies of occupation. Fasih was part of the military chain of command that experienced this transition and was one of its primary beneficiaries. In Syria and Palestine, as in Hijaz and Iraq, the situation was very different. For Lieutenant Aref Shehadeh, the transformation took place in his Siberian internment, where the Russian command successfully manipulated Turkish-Arab ethnic tensions among Ottoman prisoners.

Ihsan Turjman's diary is exceptional for its extreme positions against Cemal Pasha and the CUP leadership. We should compare it not to Arab nationalist historiography of the postwar period but to autobiographical works by contemporary writers such as Muhammad Izzat Darwazeh and As'ad Rustum. Both authors started their political careers as Ottoman decentralists and ended by joining the Arab nationalist camp. In Ihsan's circle both Sakakini (his teacher) and Omar Salih Barghouti (his friend) wrote memoirs that indicate an ambivalent attitude toward Ottoman decentralism during the war. As the war progressed, both of them began to identify with the leadership of Prince Faisal. Rustum eventually joined the Arab rebellion in Jabal Druze and became Faisal's private secretary. Sakakini escaped from Damascus after his release from jail (in 1918) and went over to the rebel side—where he was credited with the writing the Arab national anthem. For all of them the turning point was the Allied military trials of Syrian nationalists and their hanging in Beirut in August 1916.

By contrast several members of the Jerusalem intelligentsia continued to favor a settlement that would keep Palestine as an Ottoman province until the end of the war. They included Adel Jaber, who edited *al Hayat* in Jerusalem and Jaffa; Sheikh Muhammad Salih, director of Rawdat al Ma'arif; and Mahmud Jawish, principal of al-Salahiyya College. Omar Salih, in his autobiography, discusses meetings held by Cemal Pasha with Arab leaders in Jerusalem and Damascus in 1916 and 1917 to discuss a Turkish-Arab confederation.[83]

Turjman's diary contains a sustained tirade against Cemal and Enver Pashas, particularly against Cemal's failed campaign in the Suez and the Sinai desert fronts, which involved many of Ihsan's friends and relatives. A recurrent nightmare was Turjman's fear of being sent to the front. His portrayal of Cemal is contradictory. On the one hand, he depicts him as pandering to Jewish and Christian soldiers, seeking to win the support of the minorities of Syria by exempting them from military service and assigning them to clerical jobs. On the other hand, Ihsan attacks both Enver and Cemal for humiliating Jerusalem Jews and Christians by conscripting them into the labor battalions to clean the streets and undertake heavy-duty road and railroad construction. Many members of these battalions perished from hunger and disease in the backbreaking work. Contemporary descriptions are replete with tales of the humiliating impact of these battalions on the local population. One of several entries by Sakakini on this subject makes the following observation: "Today a large number of Christians were recruited as garbage collectors to Bethlehem and Bait Jala. Each was given a broom, a shovel, and a bucket and they were distributed in the alleys of the town. Conscripts would shout at each home they passed, 'send us your garbage.' The women of Bethlehem looked out from their windows and wept. No doubt this is the ultimate humiliation. We have gone back to the days of bondage in Roman and Assyrian days."[84] When he was appointed as a temporary clerk in the Jerusalem military command in charge of exemption from service, Turjman tried, unsuccessfully, to ameliorate the suffering of these soldiers.

In one episode Ihsan describes Cemal Pasha's wedding to a "Jewish prostitute" from Jerusalem as an example of his favoritism. He is referring to the commander's concubine Lea Tannenbaum, whose family was active in the pro-Ottoman Red

Crescent Society. Other entries portray Cemal as arbitrary and engrossed in his own glorification—extending work hours for ordinary soldiers and abolishing their weekly holidays on Fridays. Cemal is also seen as hypocritical, distributing sweets and slaughtering lambs for the benefit of the soldiers during public holidays yet letting them go hungry and underpaid for the rest of the year. Ihsan was particularly hostile to the CUP's cynical attempts to manipulate religion in defense of the war effort in the Arab provinces. One of several entries describes Ruşen Bey's hosting of a major party in the military headquarters in honor of Ahmad Cemal Pasha and Cemal the Younger (Mersini).

The height of Ihsan's wrath against Cemal Pasha is recorded during Cemal's campaign against the secret nationalist groups. The attack started with the hanging of two soldiers at Damascus Gate on March 30 allegedly for being spies for the British army. The repression reached its zenith in the execution of members of the Arab society and the secret "'ahd" group among Arab officers after a summary trial in Aley. But Turjman's anti-Ottoman sentiments are tempered by his positive reference to several Turkish and Albanian commanders toward whom he had great affection. Those included his commander in chief Ali Ruşen Bey (an Albanian); Nihad Bey, the chief of staff of the Jerusalem garrison (a Turk); and many Turkish officers with whom he had worked. When he was assaulted and threatened by his commanding officer (an unnamed Albanian), he sought the protection of Ruşen Bey, not from his fellow Arab officers.

Ihsan's diary is full of recrimination about Arab submissiveness in the face of Ottoman military repression. He repeatedly describes the Syrian and Palestinian people as a subservient lot *(ummatun dhalilah)* who are no match to the Turks. No proud nation would tolerate being led to slaughter and not rebel.

Although a pacifist at heart, he occasionally rejoices in Ottoman victories in Gallipoli and Kut al Amara (southern Iraq), and he describes his national identity interchangeably, sometimes writing that he belongs "to the Ottoman nation" and other times saying he is part of "the Arab nation," but never does he define himself as a member of an "Islamic nation"—a category that Cemal Pasha began to cultivate after 1917 to win Persian and Indian support to the Ottoman side. The *ulama* and sheikhs were particular objects of scorn in Ihsan's diary. Sheikh As'ad Shuqairi, the mufti of the Fourth Army from Akka, is described as a hypocrite for traveling to Istanbul with religious bodies from Palestine to eulogize the Ottoman martyrs in Gallipoli and the Dardanelles.

Only when Sherif Hussein and the tribes of Hijaz rebelled against Ottomans, with British support did Ihsan express his vindication and pride for being an Arab. "Salute to the Hijazis. May God lead Hussein to victory, so that the blood of our martyrs in Beirut shall not go in vain." But he calls the rebels the *'urban* ("Bedouins"), and he is aware that their revolt is not entirely altruistic. Among the reasons he cites for their rebellion is the fact that Cemal Pasha stopped paying protection money to the Hijazis for securing the Damascus Medina rail tracks.

The impact of this rupture in Ottoman identity on Turkish-Arab relations can be fruitfully traced from the Turkish side in another war remembrance—the memoirs of Falih Rıfkı, who was Cemal Pasha's private secretary in Damascus and Jerusalem, and a contemporary of both Turjman and Fasih (by a strange coincidence, Rıfkı, like the three soldier-memoirists, was born in 1893).[85] Rıfkı's observations are particularly valuable because he was close to the events as they unfolded and because he was a keen observer of Arab-Turkish relations inside the armed forces. In addition Rıfkı was fascinated by the dramatic ways in which religion in molded people's lives in the Holy Land. In the following observation he compares Jerusalem with Medina:

> The pilgrims in Jerusalem are no happier than the pilgrims at Medina. The people of Jesus are as hungry as the people of Muhammad and are equally doomed to live in misery. The only difference is the majestic décor of the beggar in Jerusalem. Medina was an Asiatic bazaar which has turned religion into trade goods. Jerusalem is a Western theatre which has turned religion into a play ... I thought the priests of the Holy Sepulcher were wearing false beards. When they bend down, one can see the bulge of their pistol-holsters beneath their robes.[86]

In general Rıfkı justified Cemal Pasha's campaign of repression against the Arab nationalists as a way to preserve stability and effective Ottoman administration. Furthermore he apparently believed that the use of violence was effective: "For Palestine we used deportation; for Syria, terrorization; for the Hijaz, the army. The circumspect Jews, waiting on the coast at Jaffa for the Balfour Declaration, lost no lives for its sake; not so much as an orange. The Hijaz rose in revolt, but Syria was quiet."[87] In his memoirs, he also defends the massive deportations of the civilian population from coastal Palestine, especially from Jaffa, after the British fleet established its blockade. The Jewish population especially, in his view, had to be prevented from sending intelligence to the Allies about Ottoman troops.[88]

Rıfkı makes insightful observations about the integration of Turkish and Arab ethnicity into Ottoman society. "The Ottoman Sultanate is solidly bureaucratic, but the bureaucracy here [in Palestine] is half Arab. I have not seen a single Turkicized Arab, and I have seen precious few Turks who were not Arabized.... We have neither colonized this region nor made it part of our land. The Ottoman Empire here is the unpaid watchman of the fields and streets."[89] When the author moves on to discuss the situation in Jerusalem, this notion of the *assimilating* but nonassimilated Arab becomes a source of protest against the Turkish predicament outside Anatolia. "We are lodgers in Jerusalem," Rıfkı remarks sardonically, in a manner reminiscent of Russian protestations of being marginalized in Soviet Moscow. "As all minorities in the Ottoman Empire had privileges, while the Turks had none, it was more advantageous to belong to any Muslim minority than to be a Turk."[90] These remarks may sound ridiculous to an Arab historian looking back at the era, but they reflected a serious perception of the "Arab problem" within an important contingent of the ruling Ottoman elite, and certainly by Cemal Pasha himself, who was fighting a desperate struggle to salvage the Ottoman idea as secessionist groups gnawed the peripheries of the empire. The significance of Arab integration, in this view, was that Arabs were the last element of the Sultanate (the Kurds probably did not count then) that was Muslim (in the main) and a potential ally against co-optation by the Western powers. Hence the disappointment was compounded by the Arab "betrayal." At the end the Arabs deserted the Turks; the Turks—in their campaign of Turkification—did not undermine the Ottoman idea. This perception is clear in Rıfkı's analysis. "Don't think there was an 'Arab problem' in that huge land stretching from Aleppo to Aden," he insists, " . . . what existed then was widespread anti-Turkish sentiment. Take that away and the Arabs would have collapsed into disunity."[91]

Rıfkı does not shed light on Cemal's presumed strategy of building an Arab-Turkish federation to replace the disintegrating Ottoman regime, as suggested by some Arab thinkers, like Omar Salih. But he makes clear in his memoirs that Cemal's failure was a defeat for any future Turkish-Arab dominion. Rıfkı recounts the bitterness of seeing his commander replaced in the supreme command by General von Falkenhayn:

> Cemal Pasha was unwilling to give up his Syrian dream; he wanted to return to Istanbul at the end of the war bearing the gift of a Syria preserved. Perhaps they took advantage of his weakness for pomp and circumstance; he was appointed commanding general of Syria and Western Arabia. A sort of commander-in-chief, second class [to von Falkenhayn]. . . . It wasn't Cemal Pasha that was falling; it was the province of Syria. But because it was a country with an excessive regard for rank, decorations and gold braid, it fell not as Anatolian villages fall, in silence and loneliness, but more showily and magnificently, wrapped in the uniforms of commanders-in chief, marshals and ministers.[92]

In the introduction to his memoirs, *Zeytindagi* (Mount of Olives), Falih Rıfkı refers emblematically to this problem of Turkish identity in Palestine. "*Olberg* is the German [term] for Mount of Olives. *Jabal al-Zaytun* is the Arabic. And *Zeytindagi? Zeytindagi* is just the name I gave to my book. *There never was a Turkish Jerusalem.*"[93] But of course there was an *Ottoman* Jerusalem, which Rıfkı bey was resisting identifying.

THE END OF INNOCENCE

Ihsan Turjman's diary is a long, sustained attack on the ethos of war. His stance is born not so much from an ideology of pacifism as from revulsion against the war-induced social disintegration and the loss of the earlier era of stability—conditions that he attributed to the megalomania of the new Ottoman leadership. The new politics of nationalist aggrandizement, ethnic oppression, and carnage brought an irrational and incoherent world. It produced what John Berger called "the inversion of politics." As in the European front, in Belgium, in France and in the Dardanelles, the impact of the war was seen as catastrophic, and people felt they had lost control over the future. With the earlier debate about the future of Palestine, we witnessed a sense of disorientation and a decentering from old certainties. The impending loss of empire created a sense of geographic fragmentation. According to John Berger, under these conditions of alienation, which were very similar to the situation in the Levant, "Nobody realized how far-reaching would be the effects of the coming inversion of politics—that is to say the predominance of ideology over politics." This was also the case with the European war, which ended the age of "political innocence":

> Soon such innocence ceased to be justified. Too much evidence had to be denied to maintain it: notably the conduct of the First World War (not its mere outbreak) and the widespread popular acquiescence in it . . . what in fact happened is that most people remained politically innocent at the price of denying experience—and this in itself contributed further to the political-ideological inversion.[94]

We can see this spread of popular acquiescence recorded in Ihsan's daily impressions about the progression of the war. Indeed, the world was disintegrating around him. The large-scale military impounding of grain from the peasants led to skyrocketing food prices in the city, followed by the disappearance of vegetables and meat. Women and children (most young men were already conscripted) formed long queues in front of bakeries and fought for meager amounts of bread. Famine truck every major town in Syria, Palestine, and Mount Lebanon, and as Ihsan notes, it was man-made, caused initially by the British economic blockade of the Palestine coast and later by military sequestration of food, not by scarcity. In Lebanon the famine was compounded by economic sanctions imposed by Cemal Pasha to punish nationalist leaders for their presumed collaboration with the French authorities.[95] By the summer of 1915 the locust attack reached Jerusalem, followed by the spread of cholera, typhus, and other epidemics.

Beggars began to appear everywhere. The graphic descriptions of beggars in European travel literature might cause one to assume that begging was a perennial feature of the Jerusalem cityscape. Had this been the case, however, Ihsan, who spent all his life in the old city, would not have devoted much attention to them in his diary. In fact the war led to the disintegration of family life and created an army of beggars. As in many provincial capitals of the Ottoman Empire, the very poor were catered to by a chain of endowments known as *takaya*, which provided soup kitchens and public food. In most neighborhoods people took care of their own, through confessional and kinship networks. With the onslaught of the war and the wide-scale absence of male breadwinners from poor families, the city experienced the breakdown of communal solidarities. The monthly salary of an Ottoman soldier was eighty-five piasters, hardly enough to buy his monthly consumption of tobacco. During the war tobacco was a main staple of survival and a medium of exchange among soldiers. It became a hard-sought commodity in the black market. At least twelve entries in Ihsan's diary deal with the absence of cigarettes and the crisis it represented to soldiers and civilians alike. The absence of tobacco became a metaphor (in all war diaries) for the general deprivation imposed by the war. On Friday, April 23, 1915, Ihsan made the following entry:

> Nowhere can we find cigarettes. Everybody is complaining and missing their *tutton* [Arabo-Turkish for rolling tobacco]. We have been deprived already of sugar, kerosene, and rice, but these short-

ages have not had the same impact as the deprivation of tobacco. . . . People in the city have given up on most items but now, deprived of their smokes, they are attacking the government for getting us involved in this war.[96]

Officers were given preference when new consignments of tobacco arrived, and they often supplemented their salaries by selling it to soldiers, especially if the shipment included choice brands from Istanbul, such as Samsoon and Murad.

With the economic collapse of many households, Jerusalem, like Damascus and Beirut, began to witness the emergence of a new institution: prostitution. The Ottoman military had introduced its own bordellos in the holy city to cater to soldiers. Several contemporary writings mention that the high officer corps, as well as potentates and city notables, kept concubines.[97] By the second year of the war, however, prostitution was widespread and serviced all categories of army personnel—most of whom were separated for months and years from their families and female company. On the occasion of Sultan Muhammad Rashad's assumption to the throne, on April 27, 1915, Cemal Pasha held a major party in the garden of the Commissariat for the Ottoman high brass and local notables. Fifty prostitutes were brought in from the city bordellos to accompany the officers— while the city notables brought in their wives. Ihsan expressed his shock at this mixing of prostitutes with "respectable" ladies, but also at the fact that this indulgence took place at the height of fighting in Janaq Qal'a (Gallipoli), where thousands of fellow soldiers, Arabs and Turks, were being slaughtered. Prostitution soon spread to the streets of the old city.[98]

To illustrate the depths of moral degeneration in the city, the diarist cites a case in which several well-known teachers from a public school in Baq'a were caught hosting local prostitutes in school during teaching hours. The Jerusalem governor had the three teachers (who included the religious instructor Sheikh Yacoub Azbaki) expelled from their positions. But former mayor Faidi Alami (then a member of parliament in Istanbul) intervened on their behalf, and their sentence was reduced to paying a fine of 150 *qirsh*.[99] Ihsan wrote in protest, "Teachers should be first professionals whose conduct is above reproach, and secondly, they should be equipped with knowledge in the training of children. In our case thank God both traits are lacking entirely. It is true that teachers are human beings and have needs to satisfy their basic desires, but they should exercise control over their instincts. In all cases they should never be allowed to bring women of easy virtue to their schools where children are [exposed] to these practices, and are given a bad example in ethical conduct."[100] Many poor war widows in Ihsan's own neighborhood and near Damascus Gate were seen selling their bodies for a few piasters. Ihsan met them daily on his way to work near the new gate. One evening, while he and his cousin Hasan were on their way to have dinner with Sakakini, he met a streetwalker loitering near the Austrian Hospice.

> I said to Hasan, "This poor woman, waiting for her deliverance."
> He said, "What can she do? She has to live. She makes a majidi per trick to survive." What miserable creatures, selling their bodies for pennies to satisfy the bestial needs of men. I am sure that most prostitutes would not practice their professions except for their [financial] need. Some may have enslaved themselves to men who promised them marriage and then deserted them.[101]

Ihsan expressed his compassion for the Jerusalem prostitutes in terms of general compassion for Muslim women. He had read and admired Qasim Amin's call for women's emancipation

(*Tahrir al Mar'a*, 1899) and expressed the belief that the general backwardness of Arab society was related to the confinement of women. He also called for the removal of the veil and linked the struggle for women's rights to the fight against the Turkish dictatorship of the CUP. The occasion for his comment was a department of education ban on the performance of dramatic shows in public schools that alluded to the heroism of classical Arab figures (in this case a play about Tariq Bin Ziad, the conqueror of Andalusia).[102] "We have entered into a compact with this [Ottoman] state that can only work if we are treated on equal footing with the Turkish [subject]. Now however the state has chosen to treat us as a colonized possession and the time has come to break the partnership." He adds,

> I spoke with Hilmi Effendi about the status of the Muslim woman. I told him that education is the key to her emancipation. I mentioned that the veil is an obstacle to her advancement, but it should not be removed all at once since this would harm the movement to improve her condition. I said, "How can we progress when half of our nation is ignorant? How can we live when half our bodies are paralyzed? We need to teach her, then teach her and teach her."[103]

By spring of 1915 Jerusalem, as well as the rest of the Syrian provinces, was overwhelmed by a sense of impending catastrophe. The combination of war casualties and natural disasters produced a sense of atrophy among the civilian population. "Our lives are threatened from all sides: a European war and an Ottoman war, prices are skyrocketing, a financial crisis, and the locusts are attacking the country north and south. On top of all this, now infectious diseases are spreading throughout the Ottoman lands. May God protect us." Ultimately his reaction to the accumulated catastrophes, like that of many Jerusalemites, was one of increasing indifference, almost a placidity, a response that is common to people seeking to shield themselves from impending doom. "Usually I worry about the smallest matter that can happen to me, but now with disaster visiting everybody, I have stopped caring. Since this devastation has been heaped on our lives, we cannot focus on one single calamity. One disaster overwhelms the other; and when we think of all these misfortunes coming together, we stop caring at all."[104] One year later the situation got even worse, with hunger setting in:

> Monday, July 10, 1916. Jerusalem has not seen worst days. Bread and flour supplies have almost totally dried up. Every day I pass the bakeries on my way to work, and I see a large number of women going home empty-handed. For several days the municipality distributed some kind of black bread to the poor, the likes of which I have never seen. People used to fight over the limited supplies, sometimes waiting in line until midnight. Now, even that bread is no longer available.[105]

As the carnage of war engulfed people's lives and Cemal Pasha escalated his measures against Arab nationalists, anti-Turkish sentiment increased. With the intensification of fighting in the Sinai Peninsula and Suez, more Jerusalem residents were either taken to the front or forced into labor battalions to undertake public work for the army. In September 1918 the Fourth Army issued a new order banning the stationing of soldiers in their own townships—an order that would have transferred Ihsan from his clerical work to the front in Suez. He wrote,

> I cannot imagine myself fighting in the desert front. And why should I go? To fight for my country? I am Ottoman by name only, for my country is the whole of humanity. Even if I am told that by going to fight, we will conquer Egypt [liberating it from the British], I will refuse to go.[106]

The expression "I am Ottoman by name only" must have seeped into Turjman's vocabulary from Khalil Effendi Sakakini, his teacher and mentor, who had written a similar statement in his private diary during the war. "Why do the authorities want to exile me from Jerusalem? I am not a Christian, nor a Buddhist, nor a Muslim, nor a Jew. I do not see myself as an Arab, or an Englishman, or a Frenchman, or a German, or a Turk. Above all I am a member of the human race."[107]

The lofty ideals Ihsan expresses in his diary—toward nationalism, the emancipation of women, the alleviation of poverty, and especially his amorphous humanism—were born of his prewar innocence and were unattached to any ideological commitment, whether socialist, nationalist, or religious. He was free from all ideational constraints—partly due to his lack of a rigorous educational background but also—like Sakakini and Mikhael Naimy from the same generation—due to his naïve belief in humanist concepts, which was soon to be extinguished.

But unlike the situation in Central and Western Europe, where the war ushered in the repressive apparatus of the modern nation-state, as well as the promise of social emancipation, the Syrian-Palestinian front opened up a different set of possibilities to Arab society. Instead of fostering internationalism, it gave rise to new nationalisms and an appetite for national self-determination. Instead of bringing social emancipation, it created a vivid experience of modernity, enhanced by the machinery of war and the emergence of a mass society that undermined communal solidarities. The building blocks of such a society—the press, public education, and notions of citizenship—had been evolving in Europe for over a century. But the experience of social emancipation and the emergence of a new national identity were intertwined only in concept. As we will see, they took place in the mind of the young soldier, and his generation, as separate life events.

DISCOVERY OF INTIMACY

The experience of new rhythms of daily life was at the heart of these modernities of war. We have seen that the war created a new sense of time (discreteness) and geography (the decentering of Palestine within the imperial domain); increased people's mobility through the advent of the railroad and the automobile, introduced greater discipline in military work, and conquered the night (through electrification and the positioning of guards on the streets outside the city walls). As a result, people in the city began to socialize and entertain themselves in the evening.[108] Ihsan's diary refers to daily incursions into the municipal park in Manshiyyeh, on Jaffa Road, where Ottoman military bands entertained the public. Ya'acov Yehoshua, father of Hebrew writer A. B. Yehoshua, wrote in *Jerusalem of the Old Days (Yerushalaim Tmol Shilshom),* "[The] Army Band played there twice a week conducted by a person called Kovalsky (who had a music instruments shop)."[109] In the same period Wasif Jawhariyyeh, the musician, also described Manshiyyeh as a major place of entertainment in the city. His father, Girgis, had a concession for a café there, where Wasif and his brother played their ouds. The place was particularly popular among soldiers.[110] The new sense of mobility meant that people's work and social networks began to extend beyond their townships. In discussing his marriage plans, sometime toward the end of the war, Ihsan contemplates finding a partner outside Jerusalem—a possibility that would have been unthinkable a generation earlier.[111]

Mass-circulating newspapers and popular books were also

new developments during the war. Papers were read aloud in public cafés for those who were illiterate or could not afford them.[112] In Palestine, as in Syria and Egypt, the daily press already existed, of course, but the war enhanced newspapers' circulation because people were hungry for news from the war front (Iraq, Suez, and the Dardanelles) where their family members were stationed.

Ihsan's diary reflects the obsessions of a young soldier with the care of his body and its ailments. Again he displays the strong influences of al-Dusturiyya College, which offered physical training classes as part of the core curriculum. Muhammad Salih's Rawdat al Ma'arif introduced similar paramilitary classes.[113] Sakakini was famous in his circle for his regimen of daily cold showers and rigorous physical training, and Ihsan sought to follow his mentor in this practice. Amateur wrestling was one of his Sakakini favorite pastimes, in which he engaged many of his students and fellow teachers. Ihsan himself was a mild hypochondriac, examining his body daily for symptoms of disease and expressing fear of catching one of the main epidemics that ravished Palestine during the war: malaria, cholera, and typhus. Many of his comrades and acquaintances died from the latter two diseases.

For a provincial Ottoman city, Jerusalem was well equipped with medical facilities and services. Both government clinics and mission hospitals gave Palestinians a wide choice of medical services.[114] Two of Ihsan's cousins, Hasan and Hussein Khalidi were newly trained doctors serving as medical officers in the Jerusalem area. His neighbor Rustum Effendi was an *ajzakhani* (pharmacist) and played a big role in Ihsan' crisis at the end of his life. Another doctor, Tawfiq Canaan, the famous dermatologist and ethnographer from Beit Jala, was the director of Jerusalem's Military Hospital and also a family friend. Ihsan often used his services to acquire medical leaves from army duty (and Canaan was apparently happy to oblige). When Ihsan discovered a rash on his genitals one day, Hasan (his cousin) examined him and informed him that it was probably a venereal infection (*al da' al ifranji,* "the Frankish disease"). Ihsan went into panic. He protested using the same language attributed to the Virgin Mary when she was informed by the angel of the Lord that she was bearing a child: *lam yamassani basharan* ("I was not touched by a human being").[115] And when Dr. Khalidi suggested that perhaps the rash came from "association with soldiers" *(mu'asharat al 'saker),* Ihsan threatened to commit suicide. He was particularly concerned that catching any disease would jeopardize his future chances with his beloved Suraya, the woman he intended to marry. Eventually the rash disappeared, and he was restored to sanity.

Contemporary observations indicate that homosexuality was widely practiced in the Jerusalem garrison, as in the ranks of armed forces worldwide. Ihsan was shocked when one of his commanders, an Albanian officer, took a sudden fondness for him and pursued him relentlessly. He recorded in his diary that the officer wrote him incessant letters expressing his affection and the desire to play with his hair and "kiss me between the eyes." When Ihsan rebuffed the man, the Albanian resorted to threats and became abusive. He began to visit Ihsan at his home late at night and threatened to kill him unless he yielded. Finally, in desperation, Ihsan hesitantly reported the abusive captain to his commander in chief, Ruşen Bey—also an Albanian. He was afraid of the man's retribution. At this juncture the diary abruptly ends. This episode casts dark shadows on the causes of Turjman's death, since we know from family sources that he was killed by an Ottoman soldier just before Allenby troops entered Jerusalem in December 1917.

Ihsan's diary dwells at length on his search for love. His experience is typical of young Arab men at the turn of the century. Similarly Muhammad Fasih's diary, despite its preoccupation with the deteriorating situation at the front, makes many references to a normal life with his wife (or betrothed). More women began to appear in public and to encounter men at work and in their neighborhoods. Literacy and mobility allowed for men and women to exchange letters and have chaperoned rendezvous, sometimes with their families' blessings. Romantic correspondence from the 1910s and 1920s indicates that young people were influenced by the European romantic novels they were reading and were beginning to articulate new notions of love and intimacy.[116] Studio photographers like Khalil Raad and Krikorian catered to the needs of friends and couples to exchange photographs on holidays. In these ritual exchanges, the photographs became mementos of friendship and tokens of remembrance of the beloved in periods of extended travel. The subjects of these photographs adopted their most impressive posture and dressed in their best attire, often wearing their official uniform and (for soldiers) holding a gun or a ceremonial sword.[117]

Unlike middle-class intellectuals like Alami, Sidawi, and Sakakini, Ihsan experienced a restricted and sublimated kind of love, since the object of his affections, Suraya, was unattainable. Her family was not ready to accept him, presumably because he was an ordinary soldier with few prospects of a decent income. To complicate matters she was veiled, and he was able to steal a look at her only by hiding near her house in the old city and waiting for her to remove her veil as she entered the house. On one occasion, he left his photograph with her brother, hoping that she would reciprocate. He was frustrated by the appearance of a competitor for Suraya's love—a more established and more financially secure intellectual whom he refers to as A. B. The cryptic narrative suggests that A. B. was his code for Adel Jaber, at the time a professor at al-Salahiyyeh college and a close friend of Sakakini in the Sa'aleek circle (Vagabond Party). Fortunately for Ihsan, neither Suraya nor her mother reciprocated A. B.'s overtures. But the danger remained that her father was considering other suitors. In any case Turjman's attacks on Jaber's pro-Ottoman politics were likely also a cover for his personal loathing and jealousy of the latter's overtures to Suraya.

Ihsan's love affair with Suraya, and his failure to consummate it, became emblematic of his search for a life of normalcy, which was denied to him by the war and his life in the army. His daydreams usually involved an escape from military service—going to the countryside, becoming a farmer, and settling down with Suraya. Despite his disciplinary background, or perhaps because of it, Muhammad Fasih also dreamt of a sudden escape from the military to enter into the tranquility of married life. His search for domestic normalcy was even more pronounced and explicit than Ihsan's since he was denied it altogether in the trenches. "Daydream about a happy family and congenial kids. Will I live to see the day when I have some?" (November 22, 1915); "Oh My God, will I ever have a child who will call me daddy?" (November 24); "Will I ever have a sweetheart? God, maker of heaven, earth and all the creatures that inhabit it. Please allow me to see the day when I shall taste this bliss. Otherwise my life, which has always been so sad, shall remain full of yearnings and grief" (December 4). Turjman, who had spent his entire adult life war, imagined peace in a different way—as a plateau of tranquility that literally existed in a different country (often the Swiss countryside), a vision almost assuredly borrowed from the pages of the popular romances he consumed during his desk job at headquarters. The confinement of his beloved Suraya, and his inability to reach her, led Ihsan to reflect on the condition of Arab and Muslim women in general. The new postwar era was linked in his mind with the emancipation of women (which in his mind meant their release from their domestic confinement) and the end of their physical seclusion.

The search for normalcy became an all-consuming passion for the vast majority of young men, soldiers, and civilians who experienced the military horrors of World War I. In their yearning the war's end would be the turning point for the new cherished freedoms. They also saw the end of the Ottoman era as the beginning of a new "rational" order, whose features were contested and fluid (would it be a Syrian homeland, an Egypto-Palestinian union, or simply the Arab nation?). Unlike many of his contemporaries, however, Ihsan expressed this yearning as a desire for a military defeat of his own army and the dissolution of "his" imperial state.

IMPRISONMENT AND EXILE: THE CASE OF LIEUTENANT SHEHADEH

The experience of imprisonment by the enemy and exile during World War I was another important dimension in the dissolution of Ottoman identity. The case of Lieutenant Aref Shehadeh, also from Jerusalem, is particularly relevant because of his considerable education and his early training in the imperial capital, Istanbul, before he was sent to the Caucasian front in 1915.

The late Ottoman period and the early colonial Mandates (French and British) witnessed the appearance of a type of polit-

Figure 5. Lieutenant Aref Shehadeh, Russian prisoner ID in Krasnoyarsk Internment Camp for Ottoman war prisoners, Siberia, 1915. Courtesy Institute for Jerusalem Studies.

ical advocate/public intellectual who all but disappeared during the later independence period. This type of activist was replaced by a new breed of public intellectual: the professional party activist (Ba'th, Nasserite, Syrian Nationalist, and communist) and the "committed intellectual" of the 1950s, and 1960s who was active within or on the margin of those political parties. An outstanding example of the earlier type of engaged scholar was Abu Khaldun Sati Husari (1881–1967), the Syrian theoretician of Arab nationalism and author of the seminal *A Day in Maysalun,* a treatise about the defeat of the first unitary Arab state in modern times. Husari's intellectual and political career marked, and played an influential role in, the transition from Ottomanism to Arabism. He both participated in the late Ottoman reforms and was a founding member of the CUP in 1905.[118]

What distinguished public intellectuals like Husari from their successors was their involvement in the public sphere without the benefit of mass political parties or movements. Their path of political engagement was their literacy (confined to the urban elite), their writings in nascent nationalist presses, their membership in literary societies and clubs (such as al-Muntada al Adabi, the Vagabond Café [Maqha al-Sa'aleek], and al Urwa al Wuthqa), and—for quite a few—training in Ottoman military academies and service in the Ottoman armed forces during World War I. The imperial military schools were significant conduits for establishing a collaborative network of the various ethnic communities in the Ottoman period. For a brief period (1908–14) they were also a crucible for socialization into a reconstituted Ottoman citizenship. Almost without exception these intellectuals served as public officers in the civil service of the Ottoman state and (later in) the French and British Mandate administration. During the Second Constitutional Period that began in 1908, the Ottoman bureaucracy was much more fluid than its British and French colonial regimes, and it allowed for considerable advancement by sections of the urban literate strata, at least in enabling provincial bureaucrats to belong to various political parties and to express dissident opinions. The intellectuals' membership in these government positions largely did not co-opt them into acquiescence, nor did it co-opt their role as public advocates of Arab unity, social progress, and—for quite a few— radical opposition to the central authority.

One has only to name a few such figures to recognize the disappearance of their species: Sati Husari (Aleppo, Istanbul, and Baghdad), Rustum Haydar (Baalback), Ruhi Khalidi (Istanbul and Jerusalem), Muhammad Izzat Darwazeh (Nablus and Beirut), Muhammad Dia Khalidi (Istanbul and Jerusalem), Khalil Sakakini (Damascus and Jerusalem), and Falih Rıfkı Atay (Istanbul, Damascus, and Jerusalem).

We can gain a deeper understanding of how the etymologies and trajectories of Syrian and Palestinian nationalism evolved. by examining the early career of officer Aref Shehadeh (1892– 1973), later known as the historian Aref Aref, whose public life spanned the late Ottoman, Mandate, Jordanian, and Israeli rules over Palestine.[119] (Much of what he later wrote—histories, essays, and diaries—constructed a nationalist discourse that was at variance with his activities (and utterances) before and during World War I.)

Aref spent most of the war period (1915–18) in Russian exile, and his Siberian experience sheds new light on the larger transformations taking place around him. Like Husari, Aref shared an early elite education in Istanbul, a loyal affinity for the Ottoman regime, and membership, or sympathy for, the CUP. Like Husari, he defected from his Ottoman loyalties at the end of the war to join the Syrian national movement under Prince Faisal. Both served as civil servants in the British Mandates (Husari in Iraq, Aref in Transjordan and Palestine), but whereas Husari became a main advocate and theoretician of Arab nationalism, Aref acclimatized himself to the fragmentation of the postwar

Arab East and played an active role both in creating Transjordan as a separate state and in administering Mandate Palestine.

Most of what we know about his earlier career comes from autobiographical fragments that he wrote, and later rewrote. Born in Jerusalem in 1892 he was sent by his family to Istanbul to finish his secondary schooling. He later studied literature at Istanbul University, receiving his first degree in 1913. Upon graduation he worked as a night editor in the Turkish daily *Bayam*.

In Istanbul he joined (and according to Yacoub Awdat, was one of the founders of) al-Muntada al Adabi (the Literary Forum), which was a meeting club for Lebanese, Syrian, and Palestinian intellectuals from Bilad al Sham.[120] After graduation from Istanbul University, Shehadeh was appointed as a translator in the Ottoman ministry of foreign affairs. With the eruption of the Great War he enlisted in the military college in Istanbul, and upon graduation he was conscripted as an Ottoman officer in the Redif (Reserve) Forces, and later in the Fifth Army, and fought on the Russian front. There he was captured and held three years in Siberia as a prisoner of war, before he was liberated by the onset of the Bolshevik Revolution. He returned home to Palestine by land via Manchuria and Japan, where he joined the Arab Revolt led by Prince Faisal. In Jerusalem after the war he published and edited the Faisali organ *Southern Syria*. During this period, he became active in the militant wing of the nationalist movement. The British sentenced him to death for his support of armed resistance, but this sentence was later commuted to imprisonment and exile. Aref eventually returned to Jerusalem and undertook a number of public positions, including Qa'imaqam of Beersheba and Gaza. In the late 1920s he became secretary of the Administrative Council of Transjordan, which made him a keen observer of the genesis of the Hashemite Kingdom. His unpublished memoirs of his time in Siberia (1915–18), and in Transjordan (1926–29) constitute a fabulous window to a vanished era and offer an interesting contrast to the "authorized" version of Aref's early biography, based on his postwar memoirs.[121] In turn, a comparison of these two sets of biographical texts with the historical record yields important insights into pre- and postwar events.

EARLY EDUCATION: I FOUND MY ARABNESS IN ISTANBUL

Aref Shehadeh, the middle son in his family, received his early education at the al-Ma'muniyyeh Intermediate School. On the eve of Sultan Abdülhamid's overthrow in 1909, when Aref was barely sixteen, his father, Shehadeh Ibn Abdul Rahman Ibn Mustafa Aref, a prominent Jerusalem merchant in the old city, sent him to Istanbul ("the Qibla of Arab, Turkish, Armenian, Kurdish, Greek, and Albanian youth, as he [Aref] called it") to receive his higher education.[122] In five condensed years (1908–13) he was able to finish his schooling at the Maktab Sultani, known as Namu'ah Taraqi, and at Istanbul University, where he received a literature degree in 1913. During his college years he worked as a night editor in the Turkish daily *Bayam* to support his education.[123]

In his later writings that look back at this period, Aref portrays his assertion of Arabism as a belief in a separatist future for the Arab nation. However, an examination of his earlier writings and personal papers yields a different picture. Al-Muntada al Adabi, which he belonged to in Istanbul, and which some sources say he cofounded with Abdul Karim Khalil, was a product of the 1908 constitutional revolution, and most of its members were firm believers in Ottoman decentralization—not secession—from Istanbul.[124] His enlistment in the military college, and subsequent military career as an officer in the Fifth Army (which he could have avoided by paying the *badal*), suggest that he was more than a casual believer in the integrity of the Ottoman regime. His fluency in Turkish advanced his career in the Ottoman bureaucracy but also stamped him with intellectual affinities for its Ottoman culture. About his discovery of his Arab identity, he wrote the following in his diary:

> I was not aware that I was an Arab, and that I should think of the future of my Arab nation until the establishment of the Literary Forum [al-Muntada al Adabi] in Istanbul. Of the founders I remember four names: Abdul Karim al Khalil, Yusif Mukhaibar, Jamil al Husseini, and Seiful Din al Khatib. I was registered as a member and was since then engulfed with the prevailing Arab nationalism among the students. It was then that I began to hear the words Arabs, Arabism, Nationalism, and Homeland.[125]

He wrote this passage after the war. However, the crucial transformation in Aref's career and consciousness most likely did not take place during his university years, as he professed in the commissioned biographical essay published by Yacoub Awdat, or during his Istanbul journalistic period, and almost certainly not during his work at the Ottoman foreign ministry, where he seemed to be a rising bureaucrat in the system.[126] Rather his radical break with Ottomanism probably occurred during his captivity in Siberia. In Istanbul Aref was close to the head of al-Muntada al Adabi, Abdul Karim Khalil, who was in turn affiliated to the conciliatory wing of the Ottoman Decentralization Party (ODP), which counseled unity with the CUP. We have no evidence that Aref belonged to either of these parties, but with Istanbul's entry into the war on the side of the Central powers (Germany and Austria), Khalil and the Literary Forum expressed support for the state and suspended their demands for reform in the Arab provinces lest it be interpreted as a form of secessionism.[127] As the war proceeded, however, its members began to feel the pressures of the countervailing tendencies that divided the CUP and ODP and pushed at least a section of ODP, then based in Cairo, to fight for independence from the empire.

SIBERIAN EXILE

Shehadeh had just graduated from military college when he was conscripted and sent to fight against the Russians in the Caucasian front. He was captured after a bloody battle in Ard al-Rum (Erzerum), in which most of his regiment was wiped out, with only eleven soldiers surviving.[128]

Shehadeh describes his Siberian experience in a little-known autobiographic text, *Ru'yaii* (My Vision), which he wrote in December 1918, immediately after his escape from prison camp in the wake of the Bolshevik Revolution.[129] The march of Ottoman prisoners to Siberia was deadly. According to Turkish historian Yücel Yanikdag, only one in four prisoners in one group of 800 Ottoman soldiers captured in the winter of 1915 reached their destination. The rest perished from hunger and disease on the forced march to the camps.[130] Altogether, the death rate was much higher than the rate among the European prisoners taken by the Russians on the eastern front.[131] According to Shehadeh's diary,

> We were taken to main camp in Krasnoyarsk, near the shores of the Yenisei river in central Siberia. I spent three years in a special internment camp, Wyuni Gordok, where the food conditions and cold where unbearable. The camp was surrounded by an iron fence

and barbed wire. Armed soldiers watched us day and night to prevent our escape. But also to prevent us from observing the life of ordinary Russians who were suffering from Tsarist despotism.[132]

Once the Ottoman prisoners settled in the camp, controls became more lax and recreational facilities improved. By the second year he was able to report,

> There were 3,500 prisoners in our camp. We had several fields to exercise in. One for football games, another for running exercises, and a third for other sports activities. We had a large hall in which we organized lectures and tutoring, a little theatre, and a substantial library. Later on I was able to put out a satirical newspaper, without authorization, for my fellow soldiers.[133]

Throughout his imprisonment Aref was able to maintain contact with his family through correspondence administered by the Ottoman Red Crescent Society. Letters written in Turkish and French to and from his father and brother Suleiman in Jerusalem survive. Because of military censorship (Russian, Austrian, and Ottoman), the exchanges were confined to inquiries about the family's health and mundane news about camp life. But he kept close track of developments on the home front. We learn from these letters that Suleiman was studying at al-Salahiyya College and that Aref made repeated requests for Arabic newspapers and journals to be sent to him in Siberia.[134] The requests indicate that packages were reaching Krasnoyarsk through the work of the Swedish Red Cross.

Eventually Aref was able to obtain a military pass to leave the camp during the day, arranged by a Polish officer in the tsarist army, Colonel Karol Reba, who wanted Shehadeh to teach him Turkish. This job allowed Aref to earn some money, and— for a period—to move into an apartment in Krasnoyarsk. Photographs from this period indicate that he had several Russian friends, including young women, who invited him to their homes. Several pictures show him celebrating the New Year and other occasions. Inside the internment camp he was able to study Russian and German. His German became good enough for him to translate into Turkish and publish in 1917 *Die Welträtsel* (The Riddle of the Universe) by the German philosopher and Darwinian scientist Ernst Haeckel.

Peter Gatrell, who examined studies of prisoners of war of the Central powers in Russia, views war incarceration as a window for studying the undisclosed consequences of imprisonment, including "solidarity, personal and group identity, and the psychological consequences of confinement."[135] Prisoners often saw exile and captivity as a "voyage of self-discovery."[136] This effect is evident in accounts of Arab (Syrian) prisoners. The most comprehensive study of Ottoman prison conditions in Siberia is by Yücel Yanikdag.[137] It confirms much of what Lieutenant Shehadeh wrote in his diary eighty years earlier, but it also provides a broader perspective on events inside the camps. One reason that prisoners were separated into ethnic groupings was to create work incentives. Since the Russians put most of the rank-and-file POWs to work in mines, railroads, and canal construction, they assumed that prisoners would work better in an environment of "common culture."[138]

Yanikdag gives detailed accounts of the conditions in Krasnoyarsk, the largest internment center in Siberia. Ottoman officers lived apart from, and under different conditions than, enlisted men. They were paid fifty to one hundred rubles a month, depending on their rank—a sum equivalent to what the Ottomans paid their Russian prisoners.[139] Initially there was little tension between Ottoman prisoners along ethnic lines, and their common belief in Islam seems to have had a bonding effect. Traditional Russian enmity to the Ottoman Turks, expressed by the local Siberian population, also brought the various groups together.[140] One main conflict was between elite *mektepli* officers, who had been trained in elite military schools and were the backbone of CUP, and *alayli* ("from the ranks" officers), who were demoted by the Young Turks before the war.[141] Possibly because of their religious affinity in a hostile environment, Ottoman prisoners experienced less class- or status-based friction than was common among Austro-Hungarian and German prisoners.

As the war progressed, however, two factors began to produce Turkish-Arab tensions within the prison camps. One was Russian favoritism toward Arab soldiers and officers, and the other was news of Arab rebellion in Hijaz and Syria (June 1916). The fall of Baghdad to the British and their Arab allies in January 1917 was a key factor in inciting these tensions.[142] Perhaps Russian favoritism toward the Arabs was a negative reaction to the fact that nearby Turkic Russian communities sympathized with the imprisoned Turkish soldiers, but the more likely explanation is that the tsarist government, the military ally of Entente powers in the war, was trying to cultivate the patronage of Arab recruits as part of its imperial strategy in the Middle East.

Yanikdag confirms the picture drawn by Shehadeh of the rich and versatile social activities in Krasnoyarsk and other Siberian camps.[143] Officers organized musical concerts and theatrical groups, and sports clubs and football teams, playing along national lines, mushroomed, with Hungarian, Austrian, and Ottoman teams competing against each other. Each major camp had its own library, usually organized by the Swedish Red Cross and the YMCA. Hand-printed newspapers, both in Arabic and in Turkish, circulated through the camps:

Every large camp had an Ottoman newspaper at one time. In Krasnoyarsk, for example, a paper called *Kurtulus* (Liberation) was quite popular with the prisoners. It featured not only news from home and about the war, but also articles on the ethnography of Central Asia and the history of the Turkic peoples. It seems that some of the most popular articles and editorials were nationalistic in nature, pointing to the appeal of Turkish nationalism among the officers.[144]

It is quite likely that the success of *Kurtulus*, and its emphasis on a Turkish nationalist identity, triggered the creation of *Naqatu Allah* (God's Camel), an Arabic handwritten paper published in Krasnoyarsk. *Naqatu Allah* was published clandestinely among Syrian soldiers in Siberia—"one-third satire, and two-thirds politics," in Aref's words. "How difficult prison life would be without a farcical side." He edited the paper with a fellow prisoner from Syria, Ahmad Kayyali. Forty-five issues were published between Rajab 1335 (1916) and Jamadi al Thani 1336 (1917). The paper's masthead displayed a camel lost in the Siberian tundra and announced the journal as a "literary, critical, satirical weekly" published in Krasnoyarsk and Divnogorsk (thirty-four kilometers west of Krasnoyarsk). Each issue sold for three kopeks, and a year's subscription cost one ruble. Commercial advertisements were accepted at five kopeks per line. The paper even listed an (obviously fake) telephone "number 49."[145] It is striking that Aref and Kayyali chose a Qur'anic image for their paper, given the former's thoroughly secular credentials at the time. *Naqatu Allah* refers to the miracle enacted by God when the Prophet Saleh was challenged in the desolation of the desert to produce a camel that gives milk, and God responded to his prayers in order to silence his doubters.[146] But it does confirm Yanikdag's claim that Islamic imagery was a bonding factor among prisoners, even though a minority of the camp residents (thirty out of four hundred officers) fasted during the month of Ramadan.[147]

THE BOLSHEVIK FACTOR: ESCAPE
FROM REVOLUTION OR LIBERATION?

Shehadeh's escape from Siberia was made possible by the Bolshevik Revolution. In his affidavit to Yacoub Awdat, Aref Shehadeh gives this account for his escape from Siberia (in the third person). "During the last year of his captivity news began to arrive of Sheriff Hussein bin Ali's Rebellion against Turkish rule. Aref prevailed on twenty-one of his fellow Arab prisoners to escape in order to join the Arab rebellion. They took the route of Manchuria, Japan, China, India, and Egypt through the Red Sea. During this arduous journey the Armistice was declared."[148] This paragraph is taken verbatim, with very slight changes, from his *Mujaz Siratuh* (Autobiographical Notes), published in 1964.[149] Surprisingly there is no mention here of either the Bolsheviks or the October events later in these writings.

But the "escape" story needs to be seen in the context of the chaos produced in the prison camps by the revolution, which happens to "coincide" with the Arab officers' departure from Siberia. In referring to the hardships of prison life in Krasnoyarsk in his "visionary" text written in 1918, he added the following sentence, which does not appear in any of his subsequent texts about Siberia:

> This was the situation during the era of Tsar Nicholas the Second, before the outbreak of the Bolshevik Revolution, which broke out throughout the country, and spread anarchy and fear. Matters went out of control [in our camp] and we had to start to scavenge for our food in the woods and the wilderness to secure our living. This situ-

ation continued until we received news of the Great Arab Revolt and the Insurrection of Hussein Ibn Ali against the Turks.[150]

Aref's daughter confirms in her recollections of her father's life that he "escaped when the Bolsheviks came to power."[151] She also reports that her father recalled the arrest and execution of Tsar Nicholas and his family in an area close to his encampment.[152]

In my view, Aref's omission of this point is related to his new nationalist consciousness and his break with Ottomanism, a process that began with ethnic segregation inside the camps and the publication of *Naqatu Allah*. During 1917 and 1918, administrative chaos spread throughout Russia. The situation inside the camps was even more acute as " the exiting agencies for POW relief and repatriation struggled to survive and cope with the displaced persons scattered across the disintegration tsarist empire."[153] It was in this atmosphere that the Arab prisoners escaped, or, depending on one's perspective, were liberated, to return to their homeland.

According to Yücel Yanikdag, the notion of an escape is much more complex: "When the Bolsheviks came to power, they declared the POWs free citizens and guests of the Russian people."[154] Thus many simply left and went back home. Others joined special communist units to bring the revolution to their homeland. Others yet, mostly officers, were declared "class enemies" by the new regime "and had their salaries cut and were promised only food."[155] Gatrell tells us of "factional infighting among POW radicals, some of whom threw their lot in with the Bolshevik Red Guards while others were committed to non-class militias."[156] At home, especially in Austria and Germany, authorities feared that returning prisoners from Russia would be carrying the "germs of the revolution."[157] This fear was not without foundation because the Bolsheviks began to organize special units among Ottoman (as well as German and Austrian) war prisoners to agitate for socialism.[158] Several Ottoman soldiers and exiles, such as the journalist Mustafa Subhi, joined the Bolsheviks and established the Turkish Red Brigades (Turk Kizil Alayi), which included about one thousand men.[159] But apparently very few of the Arabs prisoners joined. Aref does not even mention this group in his diary. Instead he and his comrades were determined to join the Hijazi rebellion and fight for the independence of the Arab kingdom in Syria.

Aref arrived at the Suez Canal fully five months after he left Krasnoyarsk and crossed over to what had become British-occupied Palestine. On his arrival he went straight to his father's shop in the old city. His father had ceased receiving news of his son in Siberia and was worried about Aref's fate after the October events. He had grown old and hardly recognized his son after the long absence.[160]

In Palestine Aref joined the ranks of the Faisali movement, whose aim was to establish the United Kingdom of the Arab East. He became a member of the newly formed Arab Club (al-Nadi al Arabi), a branch of the Damascus group with the same name, and headed by scions of the Jerusalem former Ottoman elite—members of the Abul Su'ud, Budeiri, Husseini, and Alami families. Its twin objectives were unity of Syria, of which Palestine was considered to be the southern part, and commitment to the struggle against Zionism.[161] Its main rival in the nationalist movement was al-Muntada al Adabi, reorganized from the remnants of the Istanbul literary club but now with the same objectives as al-Nadi al Arabi. By then, its founder and Aref's comrade, Abdul Karim Khalil, had been hanged by Cemal Pasha in Beirut. The rupture with the Ottoman regime was now complete. Both al-

Nadi and al-Muntada had active branches throughout Palestine and strong connections with the same movement in Damascus.

The Arab Club was headed by Jamil Husseini, an old comrade of Khalil Abdul Karim, as well as Fakhri Nashashibi, Boulus Shehadeh (editor of *Mir'at a Sharq*), Hasan Sidqi Dajani, and Is'af Nashashibi. It is in these two groups that the seeds of factional struggles within Palestine, between the Husseinis and the Nashashibis, originated.[162] That Aref, upon returning to Palestine, joined the Arab Club, not the rejuvenated al-Muntada al Adabi, to which he attributed the origins of his Arabism when he was a young Ottoman officer, is noteworthy. This decision probably had to do with the alliances and ideological orientations of these two nascent movements. Both Porath and Bayan Nuwaihid-al Hut suggest that the Literary Forum, which had only faint association with its Ottoman namesake (Jamil Husseini was a leading member of both), was in contact, and perhaps association, with French interests in postwar Syria.[163] In both rhetoric and programmatic objectives, al-Muntada was strongly for Syrian unity and against the dissociation of Palestine from Syria. The Arab Club was, by contrast, allied to the British forces in the Middle East. This alliance was a continuation (and perhaps an extension of) the joint struggle coordinated by the British and the Hashemites and their Syrian-Palestinian allies against the retreating Ottomans and for the reorganization of postwar Bilad al Sham.[164] In this effort, the British saw the Husseinis of Jerusalem, particularly Haj Amin, as their allies. However, within two years, when the military government was replaced by the civilian Mandate authorities, these roles would reverse, and the Husseinis would become the main oppositional group in the country, while the Nashashibis and their allies would become the balancing force of British interests in Palestine.

These reversals explain Aref's initial wholehearted involve-

ment with al-Nadi al Arabi early in 1918, and his close association
with the Husseinis. Aref's experience with Ottoman journalism
(Bayam) and with his clandestine *Naqatu Allah* in Siberia came
in handy. Together with Hasan Budeiri, he became the editor
of *Surya al Janubiyya* (Southern Syria), the organ of al-Nadi al
Arabi, first published on September 8, 1919. Both the publication's name and editorials reflected a strong unity with Syria
and an assumption that the British would support this unity.[165]
The motto of the newspaper (as well as the Arab Club), *Biladuna
Lana,* which appeared on the top of every masthead, referred to
Syria as the united homeland.

Soon however, *Surya al Janubiyya* became an instrument of
agitation against British rule in Palestine, as British intentions
for the Mandate became clearer. Aref Aref, who had adopted
his new name by now, as editor in chief, often spoke at rallies
against the Balfour Declaration. (Figure 6 shows him addressing a huge crowd at Jaffa Street on February 27, 1919, where the
main banner declares "Palestine is an essential part of Southern
Syria.") The paper was suspended several times, and an arrest
order was issued against Aref. He escaped to Damascus in 1920,
where he represented Jerusalem in the First Syrian Congress (al
Mu'tamar al Suri), which declared Faisal to be the king of "natural Syria." A military court in Jerusalem passed the sentence of
death on several nationalist figures, including Haj Amin Husseini and Aref Aref, for fomenting unrest. The sentence was later
commuted to ten years in prison.

Muhammad Darwazeh, the future leader of al-Istiqlal (Independence Party), met him in this period of hot pursuit. "I met
Aref Aref in Damascus when he, and Haj Amin, were seeking
refuge from British pursuit. He worked with us for the defense of
Palestine in the context of the Palestine Secret Society [Jam'iyya

Figure 6. Aref Aref, wearing tarbush and addressing the crowds on Jaffa Street in Jerusalem, in the first anti-Zionist demonstration in Jerusalem, 1919. Institute for Palestine Studies, Beirut.

Filasteen al Sirriya]. I sensed in him a revolutionary spirit combined with a cool and balanced judgment. He also impressed me with his command of Turkish and Arabic."[166] In Damascus Husseini and Aref helped establish the Palestinian Arab Society (which emerged from the "secret" society referred to here by Darwazeh, on May 31, 1920, under Haj Amin's leadership. Rafiq Tammimi, Mouin Madi, and Awni Abdul Hadi, in addition to Darwazeh and Aref, were on its executive committee. This was the historical moment—by most accounts—when Syrian and Palestinian politics began to take separate ways.[167] Shortly after this event both Aref and Husseini were pardoned and allowed to go back to Palestine, under a policy of co-optation initiated by the new civilian government of Herbert Samuel, the first high commissioner of Palestine.

Aref, according to Darwazeh, maintained his nationalist line but "withdrew from all political activities."[168] This is a fleeting assessment, but it is full of implications. It indicates that Aref, having concluded that the fate of Palestine was now separate from Syria's by virtue of the imperial divisions imposed by Britain and France, was now resigned to work within the system. His career took a radical break from his former occupation as a fighter for Syrian unity. This stance also placed him in a different milieu from other Arab Ottoman figures in Palestine, like Darwazeh and Awni Abdul Hadi. From then on he became a senior administrative officer in the Mandate government, becoming the district officer *(qaʾimaqam)* of Gaza, Jenin, Nablus, Bisan, and Jaffa). For three crucial years he was sent by the Mandate government to be the ministerial secretary of the newly formed government of Transjordan (1926–29), where he witnessed the formation of the new Hashemite state.

RESIDUAL OTTOMANISM

Aref Shehadeh stated in his diary that he discovered his Arabness in the Literary Forum in Istanbul, where his comrades from the Syrian provinces were debating the future of their relationship with the new regime in Anatolia. "I was not aware that I was an Arab, and that I should think of the future of my Arab nation until the establishment of the al-Muntada al Adabi in Istanbul. . . . It was then that I began to hear the words *Arabs, Arabism, nationalism,* and *homeland*."[169] His circle belonged to a number of political parties that emerged after the 1908 revolution—with most joining the CUP, but some also joining the Ottoman Decentralization Party and a small minority joining the secret al ʿahd group, which organized Arab officers in Istanbul for succession. But this new consciousness did not deter Aref from his affinity for, if not loyalty to, the Ottoman idea. He voluntarily fought for the Fifth Army on the Russian front, where he was captured and led to the internment camp in Krasnoyarsk. It was during this Siberian exile, in the company of thousands of Turkish, Arab, Balkan, and German soldiers, that he developed a separate Arab political identity, unlike the amorphous Arabist consciousness that he experienced in Istanbul. In the early period of incarceration the various Ottoman ethnic groups had considerable solidarity, sharing religious ceremonials, fasting together during Ramadan, and feeling they had a common destiny. Yanikdag describes an occasion in late 1915 when the Ottoman and German soldiers organized a tea party to jointly celebrate the military victory against the Allies in Gallipoli.[170] By the end of 1916, however, the Arab officers and soldiers began to drift away. This rupture with Ottoman identity among the Arabs was facilitated by political developments in Turkish Anatolia (primarily Turkification policies instituted by CUP's Ottoman leadership), but in this case also by three immediate factors: the camp's segregated dwellings for Ottoman prisoners by ethnicity (and the Russians' implicit favoritism toward Arab officers), the spread of clandestine publications like *Naqatu Allah* that provided a separatist platform for Arab soldiers and officers, and (most importantly) news of the Hijazi Arab rebellion and the subsequent collapse of the Ottoman fronts at Suez, Gaza, and southern Iraq (Kut al Amara). What Arab soldiers experienced as potential for emancipation of the Arab provinces from autocratic rule, Turkish soldiers saw as Arab betrayal.

According to Aref's later recollections, he had already decided to join the rebellion and struggle for a separate Arab homeland when he returned to Palestine from Siberia. Yet this rupture must have been gradual and protracted, given that a vision for a separate Arab homeland had not fully formed. And the looming "betrayal" of the French and British allies was already visible to many Arab nationalists. The defection was particularly alarming to Palestinians, who had to face the prospects of fighting separately against the Balfour Declaration. That factor alone made many Arab intellectuals reconsider their break with the Ottoman regime. But by that time the Turkish national movement had already ceased pursuing a common future with its Arab provinces. Aref's predicament was similar to that of another (and better-known) Ottomanist, Sati Husari, who was a devoted champion of Arab rights within a CUP-dominated empire. Like Aref, Husari had dual command of Arabic and Turkish and articulated the duality of Arab-Turkish identity in his early career. Unlike the champions of a reformed Islamic caliphate in Istanbul (such as Sheikh As'ad Shuqairi in Palestine) and fellow historian Ihsan Nimr in Nablus, both Husari and Aref were champions of a secular Ottoman identity that derived many of its ideas from Western liberalism (francophone in the case of Husari, German in the case of Aref). This stance produced considerable ambivalence (if not regret) about breaking with the Ottomans immediately after the war. Such ambivalence is not visible in the later writings of Arab intellectuals and political figures whose careers flourished in the prewar period—where the rupture, according to later reconstructions, was sudden and clear. Husari expressed such ambivalence about this period in a retrospective interview, when he said, hesitantly, "I was an Arab, and when the Arabs broke away from the Ottoman empire, *I had no choice but to join them.*"[171]

Nevertheless a majority of these activists retained a residual Ottomanism, largely because of language. In the spring of 1934, thirty years after Aref left Istanbul to fight on the Caucasian front and during his service as district officer in Gaza, he received a love letter from his wife, Sa'ema (Um Sufian), in Jerusalem. Um Sufian complained about her loneliness in Jerusalem and her longing to see Aref again:

I woke up early this morning. I walked around in the garden for a while. I picked up some flower and leaves. I picked up some beans to cook for myself. While I was milling around, you were always on my mind. It is your presence that makes this garden beautiful. Nothing has a taste without you. May God not deprive me of your presence, for it is you who makes my (our) life beautiful. When you left us last time I noticed that you had a little cold. I am thinking about it. Let me know about your health.

Your life's partner, who loves you with all her heart. Saema[172]

This letter is noteworthy because it was written in Ottoman Turkish, a language that had ceased to exist by virtue of the Latinization program adopted by the Turkish Republic. Aref and his wife continued to exchange correspondence in Ottoman, partly because they wanted to maintain a sense of privacy in their intimate exchanges, but equally, I propose, because it was the form of expression that they grew up with and was part of their cultural patrimony.

Aref thus belonged to a generation of scholar-politicians whose successful Ottoman careers (in his case, journalist in the Turkish press, civil servant, and officer) were radically disrupted by war. He was compelled to rethink his national identity, his future career as a soldier, and his ideological commitments as a political activist. But the rupture was not as total as his postwar writings suggest. His journalistic training in Istanbul proved to be an invaluable tool for his clandestine writings in Siberia *(Naqatu Allah)* and in his editorship of the *Surya al Janubiyya* (the organ for a greater Syrian Arab state). And the debates in which he participated in the literary-political circles of the Ottoman capital were crucial for his political struggles during the Faisali period in Damascus and for his protest against the Balfour Declaration in Palestine.

But these struggles were eclipsed by his accommodations to the new realities of the Mandate regime and by the shift he made within three short years from advocacy of Arab-Syrian nationalism to provincial Palestinian patriotism. Aref's Siberian imprisonment gave him breathing space and–paradoxically— a certain freedom in exile that allowed him to reformulate his future political options and past loyalties in a manner that was denied to most of his comrades.

WAR AND MODERNIST SENSIBILITIES

The diaries I discuss here articulate the subjective experience of war on two levels—the search for a national and personal identity and the internalization of modernist sensibilities. These two levels of awareness, which appear as an integrated discourse a century later, were clearly felt as distinct phenomena by the diarists and their contemporaries during the devastating years of the Great War. They experienced the modernist sensibilities of intimate individualism, romantic love, the possibilities of professional advancement, and movement away from the family sphere—though not necessarily from family patronage—independently from their concerns about the national predicament of Palestine. Although the two experiences were linked structurally, with one providing the context for the other, they were felt as separate struggles. While the emergence of an autonomous individualism was intense and vivid, the articulation of nationalist (i.e., extralocal) sentiments, contrary to expectations, was opaque and nebulous.

The three diaries are significant for two reasons. First, they were written by ordinary soldiers not encumbered by official accountability for their actions, except in the narrow sense of self-responsibility; second, they were written in the heat of the moment and thus reflect the language of their times and the immediacy of events as they unfolded before the writers' eyes. They are therefore unfiltered and unreconstructed by retrospective thought.

War diaries throw a new light on the new urbanities of the Arab East at the end of the Ottoman era. Lieutenant Shehadeh wrote from his Siberian exile but later revised his vision of an Ottoman identity after his escape and participation in the Faisali movement in Syria. Muhammad Fasih's battle years at the Gallipoli front and Ihsan Turjman's diary in Jerusalem's military headquarters—reflecting radically different experiences of war—shed light on the amorphous ethnic consciousness that prevailed within the ranks of the Ottoman army. Far more Arabs fought, and died, on the Ottoman side than on the side of the Arab rebellion, and they identified in varying degrees with the aims of the imperial army. Many of these soldiers were admittedly unwilling conscripts in a brutal war, but many others—if not most—identified with the Ottoman state once they were mobilized. These Ottoman leanings were especially strong after the 1908 constitutional revolution, which opened new horizons for Arab subjects. "My father could have easily sought an exemption from service for my brother Khalil—by marrying him off to a foreign resident, or by claiming him as an artisan," wrote a Jerusalemite Christian officer about his family's war experience, "but he chose to have him join the army in the prime of his life, in devotion to the state and the defense of the country."[173] But the war, and its carnage, created new realities that ruptured this consensus. Contrary to the ideological vision of nationalist historians, the debates among the urban population about the future of Syria and Palestine were highly diversified. Cemal

Pasha's attempts to create Islamic affinities among the intellectual strata (through al-Salahiyya College among other instruments) and in the ranks of his army were not an isolated phe-
nomenon and had powerful adherents. The eventual triumph
of the Arabist groups was less the result of successful agitation
among the population than of the sudden (and some would say
unnecessary) repression of the nationalist intellectuals and their
movements. The failure of the Egyptian campaign in Suez and
Beersheba also created an atmosphere of betrayal, which was
crowned by the Hijazi alliance with the British forces against the
Ottomans. But even at this late moment, there was little accord
among the Syrian and Palestinian intelligentsia and political
leadership about what should come next. While the Arab popu-
lace was restless with heavy expectations for peace and a return
to normalcy, supporters of Syrian independence were only one
current among others. For example, one contingent wanted Palestine to become part of an Egyptian union, while many others
continued to favor a decentralized Ottoman system until the last
years of the war and beyond.

Above all, World War I constituted a rupture with an earlier era. This rupture was expressed succinctly decades after the
war by an Ottoman officer *(onbaşı)* from the village of Anabta in
Palestine.[174] Officer Muhammad Ali Awad had survived fighting both on the Suez front and in Gallipoli and had returned
to Palestine. "I fought the English at Gallipoli for an Ottoman
homeland that no longer exists, and yet I continued living on
the same land."[175] Ihsan Turjman's war diary takes us to a "different country" that is hardly recognizable to our modern sensibilities a century and four wars later. In this Ottoman country,
Zionism was hardly an issue, the city defined the boundaries of
social bonds and alliances, and the new borders were defined by

the fighting fronts in the Dardanelles, Suez, and Kut al Amara. The devastation of war, however, made people question their basic assumptions about family, work, and nation. The rupture had many facets. The amorphous possibilities that existed during the war were sealed by the coming of the Mandate. Popular expectations about a future settlement were now delineated by new physical boundaries and psychological horizons that redefined the Syrian and Egyptian expanses of the empire. The city was no longer the communitarian world of its citizens but the center of a larger unit, which created a network connecting Jerusalem with Nablus, Haifa, and Jaffa. The mobility of war (conscription of soldiers and forceful transfer of citizens) gave way to the voluntarist mobility of commerce, career enhancement, and search for work. Ihsan's outrageous dream of looking for a wife outside the city now became a possibility, indeed a likelihood. No subsequent war over Palestine—and there were many—had a similar impact on the country. Even the war of 1948—which dismembered the nation, dispersed the coastal people inland, and created a nation of exiles—served to consolidate a separatist Palestinian consciousness.

The Diary of Ihsan Turjman

What Will Be the Fate of Palestine in This War?
Jerusalem, Sunday, March 28, 1915 [Gregorian],
15th of Mart 1331 [Ottoman fiscal],
1 Jammadi Awwal 1333 [Hijri][1]

Two years ago I began to keep a daily diary. But I soon neglected the routine and wrote only occasionally and then quit writing altogether. This evening I went to visit Khalil Effendi Sakakini, in the company of Hasan Khalidi and Omar Salih Barghouti.[2] Khalil Effendi read to us from his diary. It so excited me that I decided to restart my own memoirs. Our conversation revolved around this miserable war and how long it is likely to continue, as well as the fate of this [Ottoman] state. We more or less agreed that the days of the state are numbered and that its dismemberment is imminent.

But what will be the fate of Palestine? We all saw two possibilities: independence or annexation to Egypt. The last possibility is more likely since only the English are likely to possess this country, and England is unlikely to give full sovereignty to Palestine but is more liable to annex it to Egypt and create a single dominion ruled by the khedive of Egypt. Egypt is our neighbor, and since both countries contain a majority of Muslims, it makes sense to annex it and crown the viceroy of Egypt as king of Palestine and Hijaz.

Rumors abound in the street today. We heard that the English fleet has bombarded Haifa and that several English frigates crossed the Dardanelles and reached the Sea of Marmara. Even if this item is not true, it will soon be realized, since the Dardanelles have been hammered relentlessly [by Allied ships] and cannot resist the British fleet forever. The city of [illegible] fell today in Austria. This is most likely to change the course of the war and bring our deliverance nearer.

My Job with Commander Ruşen Bey
at the Commissariat
Monday, March 29, 1915

People keep inquiring as to what I do and where I work. I tell them that I work at the Manzil [Commissariat of the Fourth Imperial Army] with Commander Ali Ruşen Bey.[3] As to the first part of the question, I hesitate to answer since I am not sure what my job is exactly. If I were to say I am a clerk, I would be lying, since when I sat for the exam the officer in charge decided that my handwriting was not good enough for official correspondence. I was then assigned to a desk, to stamp and file official documents. Occasionally I am sent on errands for the Commissariat, and sometimes I take dictation. Most of the time I just sit there playing with my moustache. There are countless clerks in this Ottoman state who, like me, occupy office space, know nothing, and receive a salary at the end of each month. Such a state is bound to disappear.

More rumors today about the bombardment of Gaza by the English fleet. Another coastal village between Jaffa and Gaza was also hit.[4]

Soldiers were seen stealing wood from our land in *Karm al A'raj.* Not satisfied with dead wood, they started tearing branches

Figure 7. Amirelai Ali Ruşen Bey, the Albanian commander of the Jerusalem garrison and head of the Fourth Army Commissariat (Manzil), Jerusalem, 1915. Institute for Palestine Studies, Beirut.

from our olive trees. Who can we complain to? The officers claim they cannot control their subordinates. Of course not. Officers are busy in the taverns getting drunk; then they go to the public places [brothels] to satisfy their base needs. . . .

Heavy rain fell over Jerusalem today, which we needed badly. Locusts are attacking all over the country. The locust invasion started seven days ago and covered the sky. Today it took the locust clouds two hours to pass over the city. God protect us from the three plagues: war, locusts, and disease, for they are spreading through the country. Pity the poor.

The Hanging of Soldiers at Jaffa Gate
Tuesday, March 30, 1915

On my way to the Commissariat this morning I met Uncle Sa'd Eddin Effendi Khalili. He asked me if I had heard about the hanging of two soldiers at Jaffa Gate. They were sentenced to death by hanging, it is claimed, because they deserted their company. What is a soldier supposed to do? The army pays each soldier 85 piasters a month and expects him to survive on it. Even then, most soldiers have not been paid one matleek since the General Call [November 1914].[5] Some people claimed that these poor sods were hanged because [the Ottoman authorities] believed that they were passing on military secrets to the British. If the British government needed [military] information, do you think it would rely on such common folks *['awam]*? These soldiers can hardly write their names. How are we to believe the army?

Cinematographic Propaganda for
the Ottoman Army
Wednesday, March 31, 1915

Yesterday we were told that the army is planning to create a cinematographic show as a display of Ottoman war preparation for the Suez campaign. For this it organized a caravan of motorcars, wagons, horses, mules, and camels in Shu'fat—north of Jerusalem. I was delighted because the occasion would give me freedom to leave the Commissariat. The caravan had hardly left when I took off to Jaffa Gate, where I met Omar Salih, Jurgi [George] Petro, and Anton Mushabik at 10:30 A.M. We were all waiting for Khalil Sakakini to come to Jaffa Gate since he went to see the mayor, asking him to help in paying his military exemption fees *[badal]*.[6] Then he came and assured us that his *badal* will be paid today. Everybody was happy, and we proceeded on our walking and chatting.

The Police Attack Women in the Haram Compound
Friday, April 1, 1915

Women await the festivities and press their husbands to buy holiday clothes for them and their children, one month ahead of the feast [for the Nebi Musa festival].[7] This year will be particularly hard on them since money is scarce and the stores are empty. Often they persevere in deprivation all year for a few days of joviality during the holidays. Today I saw a number of women walking in the plaza of the Haram compound [al Aqsa Mosque]. They have waited a long time for this day when they can be free of the pressures of their husbands and homes. Suddenly I saw a throng of policemen coming in their direction. They started shouting at the women and kicking them out of the compound. The women kept moving from one corner of the Haram to another until they got fed up with the police and left the compound altogether. [8]

I pity the condition of the Muslim woman these days. Although most women on earth seem to be oppressed and despised, this is particularly the case for Muslim women. I thank God

Figure 8. Banner holders in the Nabi Musa celebration inside the compound of al Aqsa Mosque, Jerusalem, 1918. Courtesy Library of Congress, Eric Matson Collection.

every day for not having created me as a woman. I cannot imagine what I would do if I were born female.

They Wanted to Kiss My Hands and Feet
Sunday, April 3, 1915

Today was the Great Feast [Easter] among our Christian brothers. Since Christian soldiers were released for this holiday, I was asked to fill in as a deputy for the officer in charge of petitions in the Commissariat. First thing in the morning, a man came with a petition requesting that his son be sent to the military hospital. I took his petition and sent it to the registry with a request that it be approved. I then asked the petitioner to return with his son in the afternoon. Nothing happened, and he was referred to the next day. Petitioners came in great waves because these were public holidays for Christians and Jews. All of them had taken leaves from their military battalions and had come to Jerusalem to celebrate their feasts. Soon their petitions accumulated beyond my ability to process them. The poor peasants or Jews have the illusion that because I receive their papers, I am the one who makes the final decision on their petitions. Some insist on kissing my hands, and even my feet, to urge me to give them [a positive] answer. I tried to explain to them that I only file their papers and cannot do anything about them except perhaps do some follow-up. But it was useless to explain this to them. I could hardly wait until 6:00 P.M. Western time, closed my room and left, but I all evening I thought about these miserable creatures.[9]

The Government Provokes the Feelings of Jews and Christians in the Labor Battalions
Friday, April 9, 1915

Last week the flag of the Prophet was brought to Jerusalem [on its way from Istanbul to Mecca]. It was an occasion to hang public decorations and light the old city. Victory arches were raised on top of Damascus Gate underneath the slogan "Enter Egypt in Peace with the Will of God"!! The slogan was still hanging yesterday. But today the army decided to remove the banners as a result of public criticism.[10]

Rumors abounded today indicating that our military command was to form a battalion made up mainly of Christian and Jewish citizens to clean the city.[11] This morning while walking to my work at the Commissariat I came across several Jewish citizens, almost all above 40 years of age, holding brooms and cleaning the streets. I was horrified by this scene. Every few minutes a conscript would stand aside breathing from fatigue. How cruel can their commanders be? Wouldn't it be better if the military had hired a number of younger cleaners through the municipal services and solved the problem of these sods?

My New Shoes and Father's False Teeth
Tuesday, April 13, 1915

For a whole month I have been pestering my father for money to buy new shoes. Leather is almost depleted from the market, and I wanted to buy a pair of shoes before it was too late. This evening he sent after me and gave me an English pound. Whatever is left from the cost of the shoes, I was supposed to give to my grandmother, Im Ibrahim.

My father had false teeth, but his old set has begun to deteriorate, and he can no longer eat properly. I keep begging him to replace the teeth with a new set, and he nods each time. Last week he noticed that I had pain in my molars because of the way I was eating. He insisted that I go to the dentist for treatment. I can't help but see how fathers in general, and my father in particular, give preference to their children's need above their own.

At sunset I met Omar at Jaffa Gate, who was sitting chatting with my uncle Sa'd Eddin Khalili. The three of us went to town to buy a pair of shoes for me. We moved from one store to another until we reached a German store. There I found a pair of white shoes that I fancied. I bought the shoes for 15 francs, and then we walked around Jaffa Road until dinnertime, around seven *franji* time. After dinner I went to the Commissariat and worked until after ten o'clock. At home I chatted with my mother until eleven. I went to bed and slept, dreaming of my new shoes. I could hardly wait for sunrise so that I could put them on.

Soldiers Are Not Permitted to Wear White Shoes
Wednesday, April 14, 1915

Everybody at HQ kept reminding me, "Soldiers are not allowed to wear white shoes." . . . Before lunchtime the *aghlokomandati* [work commander] Muhammad Nahhas Effendi said to me, "Who told you that you can wear these shoes? I had never seen a common soldier wearing a pair of white shoes until you showed up. I strongly advise you to take them off immediately. If Ruşen Bey or Nihad Bey or any other officer sees you, he will deduct it from your salary and give you a hefty fine." In the midst of the chaos we were in, I doubted that any of them would notice, even if I wore them for the rest of my miserable life. Nevertheless when I went to have lunch. I changed my shoes to put an end to this ridiculous tirade.

At six in the evening I went to Jaffa Gate and saw Omar [al Salih]. We came across Master Khalil [Sakakini] and his wife, Sultana [Abdo], and his son Sari shopping for a hat for Sari. After they purchased the hat, we walked with Sultana back to their home at Karm al a'raj; then we proceeded with Khalil Effendi to meet an acquaintance with whom we discussed the reform of the teaching programs at his school, [al-Dusturiyya College].[12]

A Secret That Will Determine My Future
Friday, April 16, 1915

Ruşen Bey issued an order today declaring that work will be suspended in the Commissariat every Friday between eleven o'clock *franji* and three in the afternoon. At eleven I went to al-Dusturiyya College. Miss Milia [Sakakini] was there, as well as [my friends] Jurgi Petro, Anton Mushabik, and Musa Alami.[13] At

Figure 9. Sultana Abdo, wife of Khalil Sakakini, Jerusalem, 1908. Ihsan had a secret crush on Sultana and expressed it in coded entries in his diary. Courtesy Institute for Jerusalem Studies.

eleven thirty Jurgi stood up to leave. He took me aside and said, "I will tell you a secret that will determine your future." He said he is not in a position to reveal it at the moment, but perhaps later on he will disclose it. So I let him go.

In the afternoon I took Jurgi aside and insisted that he talk. After some resistance he said to me, "Do you love lady T.?" I said, "What business is it of yours? What exactly are you driving at?" He then began to tell me the story: "A. B. tried to request the hand of T. in marriage.[14] He befriended her brother and visited the family regularly in their home. When T. became aware of his intentions, she rejected the offer entirely. The family nevertheless has not given him a final answer with the hope that she might change her mind."

Ever since I was a young man, I have been hearing that T. will be my future partner and that I will be wedded to her, and now these bastards want to compel her to marry someone else. Damn this world.

This whole episode left me in total disarray. I went again to Jaffa Gate and met with Afteem Mushabik. We strolled and talked about government policies during the war and about the Garbage Battalion that was being formed.[15] I objected to these measures [of forcing conscripts to collect garbage] on two grounds: first, employing workers directly to undertake the work of garbage collecting would be much more efficient; and second, this solution would have avoided the wrath of these miserable creatures who were forced to collect garbage against their will. I am sure most of them would be very happy to pay a fine in lieu of undertaking this sordid service.

Later I reconnected with Jurgi Petro and had him finish the story he had started earlier. He said, "You told me, Ihsan, once that you had intended to marry T. Hanim.[16] Recently I heard that A. Effendi intended to ask for her hand but that she is totally uninterested. She has been known to mock him and make fun of the way he walks." Then he gave me further reassurance. He said that when I was conscripted last year and was sent to serve in Nablus, she and her mother were depressed, and when I was relocated to Jerusalem, she was relieved.

When I heard this story, I felt assured that she was still in love with me, and I forgot all my sorrows. Still I was uncomfortable with the idea that A. B. was pursuing her. She might eventually submit to her father's pressure and marry him. Jurgi told me that this Friday A. B. is visiting the family with some dignitaries in an attempt to win her over. But I know that T. is an educated woman, and she will not be easily pressured by her family.

I only see my future happiness with her. I have loved her since we were very young. I can recognize her anywhere among thousands of veiled women, from her demeanor and her contours. At the end of our discussion Jurgi tried to calm my nerves by assuring me that A.B. is a corrupt crook and a degenerate. I differed with him, however, and insisted that he is simply ignorant. We kept talking until seven thirty in the evening; then I went home for dinner. My family was upset because I had not shown up during the day as usual. I therefore decided to skip working in the Commissariat and to stay with my father tonight. I stayed up and could not sleep until after 1:15 A.M.

A Disagreement about How to Fight the Locusts
Saturday, April 17, 1915

... At 4:00 P.M. a number of men and women gathered in front of the Commissariat to hear a performance by the Izmir military band. It was on tour to raise morale for the war effort. This is one of the best orchestras in the Ottoman provinces. I heard today that the leadership has decided to attack Egypt on the 5th of May.[17] This from a friend who heard it from a senior officer. I have grave doubts about this.

Later Farid Bey Husseini came, and we went together to hear the Shami Band in the Manshiyyeh Gardens on Jaffa Road.[18] I was very depressed and was unable to say a word. As we hit the street I saw Ruşen Bey in his motorcar for the second time today. I was hoping he did not see me since I was strolling during working hours. But the Bey is a good man, known for his leniency. After sunset I went with Hasan [Khalidi] to the Haram, where we met with Sadr [Eddin Khalidi].[19] We discussed the locust attack. They both took the position that the government should not be compelling citizens to destroy the locusts, but I disagreed with them since the scale of the attack has been massive this year.[20] The government had issued an ordinance compelling all citizens between the ages of 15 and 60 to collect 20 kilo[grams] of locust eggs. I believe this is the right thing to do. Those who do not comply should pay a fine for each uncollected kilogram. My two companions were stubborn and disagreed.

Spying on My Beloved T.
Sunday, April 18, 1915

Today was payment day. I received my 85½ piasters.[21] I also received Mahmoud Ghneim's salary, which I still have. Now he owes me 90 piasters since he gave me 4½ piasters to collect his pay and take one French pound instead.[22] . . . After work this evening I decided to pass by T.'s house to catch a glimpse of her, but she did not show up. After dinner I called on my brother Aref to see what he did with the hat. I had asked him to pass by the hatmaker Ishaq Leon to see if he had sold the hat I had placed a deposit on. It turned out that he still had it, so Aref brought it home. I looked very elegant. I decided to take a picture wearing the hat with my military uniform. The story of this hat is that Hasan and I decided that each of us would buy a hat and encase it with military cloth. But when my father saw the hat, he forbade me to wear it. Slept at 11:30.

English War Planes Attack Jaffa
Tuesday, April 20, 1915

After breakfast I went to work at the Commissariat until 12 *franji* time. In between I read *The History of Civilization*, translated from the French by Muhammad Kurd Ali (part one). I had made a commitment to myself to finish reading this book by the end of the month. Very unlikely considering how lazy I am. After lunch I took my letters received during my college days and while serving in the army when I was stationed in Nablus and began to file them. My father came and gave me 4 Ottoman pounds and 1 English pound for the purchase and delivery of three canisters of ghee *[samn]*, which he had bought from Abul Hassan Tayyan. I handed the money to his son Hassan. But earlier I had mentioned to my father that it would have been better had he bought one canister of kerosene and two canisters of ghee. He did not like what I said and kept his silence.

At 5:15 my cousin Hasan Khalidi and I met near the Manshiyyeh Gardens. He had with him Ali Abbas Ja'uni, and Abdul Rahim Tubji, son of Haj Hussein. We strolled along Jaffa Road. I could hardly say a word, since all the time Hassan was talking with Ali and with Abed about Zionism, a sort of mindless talk. Ali is a double-faced hypocrite, for he and his kind are basically with the Zionists. He said that if the Zionists need any favors from government departments, they take along their ladies, if they happen to be attractive. He himself said that if a beautiful woman comes in the company of her husband, or father, or brother, he gives preference to her petition. And this from a man who claims to be critical of Zionism. I have begun to despair about this situation.

At 7:15 P.M. we all went home. I asked Hasan if he had received any news. He said that an English plane had flown over Jaffa and sprayed the city with leaflets and disappeared. Then he told me that when Cemal Pasha, the general commander, was visiting in Gaza, English planes raided the encampment. We still do not know what the casualties were.

Hasan is rather optimistic. He thinks that within 20 or 30 days the British will occupy the country. I differ with him on this matter of timing. I believe that this war between us and the English and French, as well as the Muscovites [Russians] will last 40 months at the very least. It is true that our army cannot go back to fight in Suez again, after what it saw of British ruthlessness. But I do not think we will see the end of it until the European war is over. We need peace badly. The economic crisis is deepening, and it will not allow us to pursue this war further. Not much is left.

"The Donkey" Has a Field Day with the Ottoman Leadership
Wednesday, April 21, 1915

My father brought two issues of *al Himara* [the Donkey] newspaper today.[23] I came across the following item in the satirical page:

The Condition of Our Statesmen: Arabs and Turks

Tal'at Bey: I am the slave of time, but behold I will be its master.

Enver Pasha: We are a nation that have no fear of death . . .

Ahmad Cemal Pasha (commander of the Fourth Army and leader of the Egyptian campaign, minister of navy): Cavalry and night and the desert are witnesses to my bravery . . . and so is the sword, the pen and the spear.[24]

What kind of irrelevant trash is this? What are they saluting Cemal for? For his cowardice on the Egyptian front? I was told by one of his companions in the Suez campaign that when the battle was heated on the front, he went to the outlying trenches and started playing with his beard while trembling. One of his lieutenants, Nu'man Khalidi, asked him in French, "Would you like to eat, Pasha?" and went and got him some biscuits. The Pasha took the biscuits from him and said, "My son do you think

I can break this stuff and eat it?" I am not sure why people get worked up every time Cemal is mentioned. For his persistence in the Egyptian campaign? For his defeat at the front?

For a whole week we have ran out of *tutton* [tobacco] in Jerusalem. I had made some arrangements to buy a supply of Tetley Sirt, but it is all gone.[25] I have only one day's smoke left. I am trying to get some smuggled *baladi* [local] tobacco, even though I have to get used to smoking it.

The Garbage Battalions
Thursday, April 22, 1915

An English plane threw leaflets over Ramleh this morning. I heard that one of our planes crashed between Hafeer and Ibin, but [I have] no concrete news.[26] A small distance separates Hafeer and Ibin, yet the pilots manage to destroy their plane, while we rarely hear of English planes crashing. This can only be attributed to one of two reasons: badly trained pilots or badly maintained engines. Isn't it time for us Ottomans—or I should say "them Turks"—to leave this farce behind us and conclude a peace agreement?

The police yesterday arrested a number of Christian notables for attacking government policies. Those included the sons of Jiryis Sa'ideh, Saba and his brother, Hanna Ayoub, and Hanna Salameh, plus others whose names I did not recognize. I only heard the news this afternoon and was very sorry for it. This behavior can only be characterized as vindictive. Why would the government want to open another front against the Christians and perhaps some Jews?

The Labor Battalion was finally established, made up primarily of Christians, Jews, and very few Muslims (not more than 20). Then they announced the Garbage Battalion *(taboor al zabbaleh)*, which had no Muslims in it. This is vengeance indeed. The next step would be to start accusing people of espionage. The first to be accused and exiled will be the Christian citizens. A few days ago we had an order at the Commissariat to prepare a list of all the Christian residents, but the order was never carried out.[27] Are they assuming that the Christian citizens are less patriotic than the Jews?

The Locust Tax Is Imposed on the City's Residents
Friday, April 23, 1915

... The tobacco supplies were depleted in Jerusalem. Nowhere can we find cigarettes. Everybody is complaining and missing their *tutton.* We have been deprived already of sugar, kerosene, and rice, but these shortages have not had the same impact as the deprivation of tobacco. How strange! People in the city have given up on most items but now, deprived of their smokes, they are attacking the government for getting us involved in this war.

I borrowed a few cigarettes of my mother's favorite brand, Samsoon. She had managed to horde a few packages. This should hold me until new supplies arrive. I emptied two cigarettes and rolled them into three to economize. May God forgive those who got me hooked.

At home I heard that the government had issued new regulations for the locust campaign. Rich people now have to pay one Ottoman pound. Those with middle income pay 60 piasters, and poor people pay 30 piasters. I think the authorities did well with this edict (even though I hate them) by spreading the responsibility of collecting locust eggs on everybody and giving the option of payment [of a fine] to those who do not choose to collect. For the locusts do not discriminate between rich and poor.

But the authorities forgot to provide for the lodging and feeding of the people who decide to get involved in this campaign.

My aunt's illness has become grave. She is old, and there is no hope for her. Diseases [cholera] have spread throughout the city. Many of those infected were moved to the city's hospitals and clinics, and their homes are being sprayed. But there aren't enough doctors and medicines. Abdul Hamid Khalidi was struck by a deadly disease—I was told tuberculosis. The animals in the city were also hit, and today a large number of cows were said to have died of the cow disease *[al da' al baqari]*.

It started to rain in the afternoon. All the time I think of T. and imagine her in front of me. Whenever I remember Jurgi's words to me last week—that she loved me—I am in seventh heaven. But will I ever get to marry her? I want to know about her every movement. I often pass in front of her house in the hope that I will catch a glimpse of her. She can always see me in my portrait, which I left with her brother, but how will I get her picture?

The Shameful Behavior of Our Officers
Sunday, April 25, 1915

I was told by a friend who arrived today from Jaffa that an American ship docked at the port with a shipment of rice and sugar (and other supplies) for distribution to the civilian population. The [Ottoman] authority was negotiating for half the material to be distributed to the civilian population and the other half to the military forces. The captain of the ship refused this and threatened to leave the port. Now I am told that the debate is over how much customs this ship should pay. My friend told me that Cemal Pasha sent a memo to the chief of excise in Jaffa ordering him not to levy any customs on this ship. It turns out that

Figure 10. Cemal Pasha (center) with members of the Ottoman parliament visiting Jerusalem, 1916. Courtesy Library of Congress, Eric Matson Collection.

the shipment was sent from American Jews and non-Jews with the proviso that two-thirds of the foodstuff be distributed to the Israelites [Jews] and the remaining third to other citizens. I am not sure why the English allowed this shipment to get through [the blockade]. The future is bound to uncover this secret.[28]

Both Cemal Pasha [the Great] and Cemal the Little *[Küçük]* were invited for dinner at the Commissariat.[29] The cost, I am told, was over 30 Ottoman pounds. Yesterday HQ sent several military vehicles to Latrun to bring alcoholic drinks. More than 100 officers were invited, and the military band played throughout the meal. It's hard to take seriously Cemal Pasha's (and his retinue's) claim of devotion to Islam and of wanting to liberate Muslims from the British yoke. Every day we read a circular warning soldiers and officers against frequenting cafés and beer halls *[bira-khanat]*, upon threat of imprisonment and expulsion from service. All this while the commanders are swimming in debauchery and drunkenness.

At about five this evening two battalions marched in front of the Commissariat. What a pitiful sight. Young men, tall and well built but totally exhausted from their horrific experience [at the front]. They were wearing rags, many of them limping and wearing one shoe, or no shoes. Most members of the two battalions were Turks who had just arrived from Ibin, the ultimate hellhole of human misery.[30] And they were supposed to liberate Egypt.

The Shooting at Cemal Pasha and His Entourage
[same day]

Hasan K[halidi] came to visit around sunset. We went out for a stroll. He told me the following story: While Cemal Pasha and his entourage were driving from Gaza to Khan Yunis, they were shot at from the direction of the British fleet at sea. Cemal Pasha, our great leader, the liberator of Egypt—that is to say, our leader toward the abyss of destruction—lost his mind. He kept shouting, "There is a spy among you who informed the British that I was passing from here"!!!

After dinner Hasan and I went to visit Professor Khalil Effendi Sakakini. We met there with Sheikh Abdul Qadir Mughrabi, Is'af Nashashibi, Hilmi Hussaini, Haj Amin Husseini, and Ishaq Effendi Darwish.[31] Our talk was almost exclusively about the constitutional movement. Sheikh Mughrabi told us about his prison days. Then we discussed the works of the late Sheikh Muhammad Abdo and the works of Qasim Amin.[32] We all felt the loss of these two great authors.

Today most shops were closed since most people were out collecting [destroying] locusts' eggs. I did not go to the Commissariat this evening but stayed instead in the professor's house until 10:00 P.M. We heard that HQ will start mobilizing those born in the years 1310, 1311, and 1312.[33] God have mercy on us, they must have gone mad. I went home at eleven and slept an undisturbed sleep.

Jerusalem Whores Celebrate the Anniversary of Sultan Mehmet Rashad
Tuesday, April 27, 1915

Ahmad Cemal Pasha issued an order today, in celebration of the anniversary of Sultan Mehmet Rashad V's ascension to the throne, to distribute mutton and sweets to members of the armed forces. He also ordered the illumination of public buildings. This was followed by another circular issued by Ruşen Bey canceling the very same order since not enough rice could be obtained from the depots. It seems that rice and meat can always be found for the officers. It is only we the soldiers who are bypassed every time. Another circular was issued today reducing by one-third the kerosene provisions for soldiers.

A big party was being prepared at the Commissariat, to be presided over by the two Cemals and Ruşen Bey and other senior admirals and officers. We were ordered to extend electric lights and decorations in the Gardens of Notre Dame de France.[34] The whole city was lit by kerosene lights.... In the meantime we heard that while Cemal Pasha's aide-de-camp [*yawir*] was on his way to Nablus, his car broke down near the village of Shu'fat. The vehicle was attacked by the peasants of Shu'fat, who stripped the car and robbed his *yawir.*

To celebrate the anniversary a number of notables and their ladies were invited to Notre Dame. An orchestra performed while liquor flowed. A number of Jerusalem prostitutes were also invited to entertain the officers. I was told that at least 50 well-known whores were among the invitees. Each officer enjoyed the company of one or two ladies in the garden compound.

While this was happening, our brothers were fighting in the Dardanelles. We just heard that the English have made a major landing in Janaq Qal'a [Gallipoli] and that we have taken 4,000 of their prisoners. Our officers here are celebrating, but God knows the condition of our soldiers at the front. When I exited the main entrance of the Commissariat, I saw the invitees arriving in droves, entering through the gate lit by electricity. On the door was a huge sign saluting our sultan. I suddenly became despondent and very sad for our condition. I stayed with Jurgi Petro until 8:30. We discussed several themes, but mainly the best way to improve the condition of Muslim women. I told him that the best service we could provide for society after this war would be to open a number of schools for women. I went to sleep just before midnight.

When Commander Ruşen Bey Is Drunk, All Work Is Suspended
Wednesday, April 28, 1915

Went to work this morning and found that Ruşen Bey did not come to the Commissariat, presumably because of headaches incurred at yesterday's party. He spent all evening drinking champagne and wine and flirting with whores. As a result all work was disrupted. Where else in the world would such a thing be allowed to take place?

At 5:30 P.M. I went for a stroll with Hilmi Effendi Husseini.[35] En route we saw Nihad Bey, deputy chief of staff; Rida Shawqi, head of the registry; and Tahsin Bey, the attaché at military headquarters, swaying left and right from intoxication. They also did not show up for work. God knows where they were— most likely drinking and whoring again.

Then we stopped to talk with Sheikh Muhammad Salih. He said that the Jerusalem director of education sent a circular banning the theatrical performance of certain plays in [public] schools. The order was very stern and banned in particular the ballad *Tariq Ibn Ziad* and several other Arabic plays whose titles I forget.[36] What hypocrisy! While Cemal Pasha distributes patriotic leaflets singing the praises of historical heroes, including Tariq Ben Ziad, and while the directory of education has been encouraging the performance of patriotic plays—here comes the director of education issuing an order banning the performance of plays that teach true patriotism. What do they want from us? Are they aiming for the Turkification of all groups?

Veiling and the Status of Muslim Women
[same date]

I spoke with Hilmi Effendi about the status of the Muslim woman. I told him that education is the key to her emancipation. I mentioned that the veil is an obstacle to her advancement, but it should not be removed all at once since this would harm the movement to improve her condition. I said, " How can we progress when half of our nation is ignorant? How can we live when half our bodies are paralyzed? We need to teach her, then teach her and teach her. It is impossible for us to reach the status of civilized nations if only our men go to school. Before teaching our children, we need to teach our women." We said goodbye and each went to his home. I slept at 11:00 *franji* time.

An Encounter with a Prostitute
Thursday, April 29, 1915

Leaving the Commissariat, I met a soldier who told me that Hasan [Khalidi], my cousin, was waiting for me at Manshiyyeh Gardens. There I found the night officer sitting at the café—I walked close by the wall so we wouldn't see me, and I slipped into the Manshiyyeh. How I debase myself in this job! All of the soldiers have to be on the lookout for other officers in their daily routine. Soldiery is nothing but a school for debasement and slavishness.

At 7:30 I went with Hasan to visit Khalil Effendi. On the way we came across a prostitute loitering by the Austrian Hospice. I said to Hasan, "This poor woman, waiting for her deliverance." He said, "What can she do? She has to live. She makes a majidi per trick to survive." What miserable creatures, selling their bodies for pennies to satisfy the bestial needs of men. I am sure that most prostitutes would not practice their professions except for their [financial] need. Some may have enslaved themselves to men who promised them marriage and then deserted them. Then they found that they could not survive without prostituting themselves. Women's misery is caused only by men. May God have mercy on our youth.

A Meeting with Rustum Effendi Haydar
[same date]

We arrived at the professor's home. We met two men at the door; one I recognized as Is'af Nashashibi. The other, Hasan told me, was Rustum Effendi Haydar, the head of the Arab Sultani Office in Damascus.[37] He is an enlightened man who loves the Arab nation and the Arabic language. He was brought to Jerusalem to teach at al-Salahiyya College.

When we entered the living room, I saw Hilmi Effendi Husseini and his brother Jamal.[38] As the discussion progressed, Professor Khalil asked Rustum Effendi about conditions in Anatolia and wondered whether or not the Anatolians are more advanced than we are. He responded with a great deal of eloquence, indicating that the situation in Syria and Palestine is far superior. Most regions in Anatolia have not yet seen the steam engine or railroad, and there is a great deal of ignorance. We asked him if many of our students are in Europe. Unfortunately not, he replied. Not more than 15 or 16 students. Out of 500 students who applied three years ago, the government gave scholarships to 3 Arab students to study in Europe. Two years ago it sent only two students.

We also spoke about the need to reform the Arabic language and the gap between the written standard and the colloquial dialects. Such a gap is causing great damage, the like of which exists in no other language. Hasan objected and insisted that this situation exists in most languages.

Stealing Food from Camels— Our Soldiers Massacred in Suez
Monday, May 2, 1915

When I entered the Commissariat today, I found a young sergeant who had arrived recently from the southern front and who was talking about the horrific conditions at the front. He was attached to a platoon in charge of transporting ammunitions in the [Sinai] desert. His platoon ran out of oat feed for the pack camels. The officers ordered the soldiers to pulverize their biscuit rations *[busqumat]* and feed them to the camels. The camels resisted this food but were compelled to eat it. An officer was detailed to guard the feeding process lest the soldiers steal the camel feed, but to no avail.

Figure 11. Ottoman Camel Corps near Beersheba, 1915. Courtesy Library of Congress, Eric Matson Collection.

Then he told me the details of the attack. He said Cemal Pasha ordered the soldiers to fill the ferries at dawn and move to the western bank of the [Suez] canal. He ordered that not one shot be fired before they reached their destination. To ensure this, he disabled their guns. Once the attacking soldiers were in the water, the English saw them and began to fire their machine guns. The idiot Cemal thought that our soldiers could make it quietly to the other side and then establish a temporary bridge that could accommodate the heavy guns, the camels, and the rest of the platoon before they could be detected by the enemy. His ignorance is limitless.[39]

I asked the sergeant about the casualties. He said that the Shami [Syrian] soldiers suffered the highest casualties—about 150 soldiers in that battle, 95 martyrs from the city of Nablus alone.[40] He saw the English machine guns obliterating 70 of our soldiers in one boat. He also told me of many atrocities that I will not record here. . . .

When the railroads were extended toward the canal, the last post was named after Cemal Pasha. I said to myself, *Subhanallah* [Praise to God], how appropriate to name the most desolate corner on earth after Cemal, where only the beasts roam the land. This will ensure that his name will be cursed forever.

The agencies reported today that the British submarine 12–25 attempted to penetrate into the Sea of Marmara. Our ships intercepted it and drowned it. Two English officers and 29 seamen were captured.

The Insolence of Cemal Pasha
Thursday, May 6, 1915

Commander of the Fourth Army and Minister of the Navy and Military Commander of All Syria (these are some of his many titles) Cemal Pasha the Great ordered today that lamb meat and sweets be distributed to all soldiers, since it is al Khader [St. George] day, celebrated by our Christian brothers. I fully support this gesture since soldiers should be feasted every now and then in these days of deprivation. What is more important is that it honors our Christian soldiers, and there are many of them among us, who should feel that they are treated equally with their Muslim comrades. But I am not sure why Cemal took this step only this year since Christians have been mobilized on a large scale for the past four or five years.[41] My feeling is that he took this step to endear the Christian soldiers to him and to create the illusion that there is no difference [in the armed forces] between Christian and Muslim during holy days, as in normal times, even though in fact there is a great deal of discrimination.

As I was leaving the Commissariat, automobile sounds accompanied by a commotion came from behind me. It was Cemal

Pasha, his chest overloaded with golden medals, accompanied by his personal aide. What a disgrace! Does he feel no shame for what he has done, and for all the defeats he has led us into? I will never forget what my father said one day: "If you search the whole planet, you will not find somebody more insolent."

Misfortunes Visit Us All at Once: Locusts, War, Inflation, and Diseases
Sunday, May 9, 1915

I write this with my mind totally preoccupied. I cannot think of anything except our present misfortune. When will we finish with this wretched war, and what will happen to us next?

Our lives are threatened from all sides: a European war and an Ottoman war, prices are skyrocketing, a financial crisis, and the locusts are attacking the country north and south. On top of all this, now infectious diseases are spreading throughout the Ottoman lands. May God protect us. I can hardly walk in the streets and talk to anybody for fear of facing these misfortunes. Usually I worry about the smallest matter that can happen to me, but now with disaster visiting everybody, I have stopped caring. Hasan told me today that the Dardanelles are about to fall.

On the Road to Nebi Samuel
Monday, May 10, 1915

As soon as I woke up this morning, I heard that Abdul Wahhab Effendi Fitiani has died. I went to the Commissariat and applied to my officer for a leave to attend the funeral. While waiting I sat down and read from an English book, *What a Young Man Should*

Know. I read the chapter titled "Choosing a Wife"—which I found very illuminating.[42]

I then went to the Haram compound with my father. Two men sat next to us and babbled politics for half an hour with a great deal of arrogance. They were full of praise for the Turks and praised the German and Austrian forces to high heaven. They insisted that their combined forces will finish the English and their allies in no time. What nonsense, I thought. To think that the British fleet filling the seas, together with the French and the Muscovites, can be defeated that easily. For if they [the British, French, and Russians] decide to mobilize all the able-bodied men in their countries, they can certainly bring to the front a fighting force equal to half the people of Germany.

In the afternoon I attended the funeral at the Haram compound. Then we proceeded with the coffin to Mammilla, accompanied by my maternal cousins Sadr Eddin and Hasan Khalidi.[43] I did not go back to work that day but went with Hasan to the Khalidiyyeh Library.[44] He read to me a little; then we decided to go for a stroll to Jaffa Gate, and from there we walked on the road to Nebi Samuel.[45] I was very relaxed, and my body came back to life after a week of rot. En route we saw an old man from the American Colony walking briskly, half an hour away from the city. He stopped every now and then and checked trees by the road—as if he were looking for something.

We went back home at around 7:00 P.M. I dined and went to the Commissariat, where I heard the shocking news. Nihad Bey, the deputy commander, said that plans are afoot to abolish the Jerusalem Commissariat. If this is true, it could be a sign that the war is near conclusion, for we need the Commissariat to feed and bring munitions to the soldiers. Could the hour of deliverance be near? Yet I was overcome with fear that if the Commissariat is abolished, we will be sent to the platoons at the front. I went home thinking of this development and could not sleep.

Teachers Bring in Prostitutes to Their Schools
Wednesday, May 12, 1915

This noon a senior administrative officer in the Fourth Army committed suicide, for reasons unknown, while he was in hospital. Rumor has it that he was caught pilfering thousands of pounds from the treasury. Others say that he had personal problems. What madness. In the afternoon his cortege passed in front of the Commissariat in a huge procession. Soldiers and military police marched with their guns lowered in salute, preceded by the police. Behind them came the chief army commanders, including the two Cemals—Cemal Pasha, commander of the Fourth Army; and Cemal [Marsini], commander of the Eighth Army; as well as Trumer Pasha and other dignitaries. I should add that while all this was going on, the military band stationed at the Commissariat was playing solemn funeral music, but as soon as the procession left HQ, the band began to play popular Turkish tunes! How disrespectful can it be? This is a sign of the level of degeneracy this state has fallen into.

At 5:30 I left the Commissariat and went to see my father. He told me that the inspector of education for the Syrian districts came to the Baq'a Office of Education two days ago and questioned the staff about two prostitutes who were seen on school premises. It transpired that teachers from the local school were involved. These were Kamal Khatib, Sami Khatib, Zuhdi Alami, and Sheikh Yacoub Azbaki. When the inspector verified the incident, he presented a report to the director of education, who in turn forwarded it to the district governor. The latter ordered that the teachers involved be expelled from their positions. The [parliamentary] deputy from Jerusalem, Faidi Alami, intervened and had the directive softened. Eventually the teachers were fined by a salary cut of 150 qirsh.[46]

I find it incredible that a teacher, charged with the moral and intellectual upbringing of our students, finds it possible to bring prostitutes to school. What lesson in ethics does this teach our youth? I walked home with my father, bid him farewell, and then walked to Jaffa Gate. At the entrance to the court I saw Sheikh Mughrabi. He had asked me to lend him the second volume of *Tafseer al Zamakhshari*.[47] He had borrowed volume one over ten months ago and now wanted me to go home and get him the second volume. I hate to lend my books to people, knowing well that they will not return them.

I went to Jaffa Gate again and met with Sakakini, and stayed with him until 6:30 P.M. He begged me to go to THE SULTANAH and inform her that he will not be able to pick her up.[48] He also begged m . . . . [illegible]. I abided by his wishes and went there feeling giddy and delighted.

An Unintended Pleasure
[Wednesday afternoon]

This must be one of the happiest days in my life. I can hardly believe that this is not a dream. For I came across my beloved and (I hope) my future partner *[sharikat hayati]*. She was standing in front of her house chatting with one of the neighbors, with her veil lifted. When she saw me, she slowly lowered her veil but kept chatting with her friend. Beneath the veil I saw a shining moon and a beauty that is without parallel. I wish I were a poet so that I could compose a stanza for this occasion. How happy I will be to marry her. I have met many women in my life—European and American, Muslims, Christians, and Jews—but never encountered a lady with such graces. Glory be to your creator. Until today I loved her only in my mind's eye. I would recall her image from my younger days, when I knew her as a child. But now I realize that her beauty far exceeds the image I have had of her all these years. I stood there paralyzed, staring at her visage and the light that emanated from her. It was already early evening when I saw her, and the dusk light had set in, but that was enough for me. I used to pass by her house daily, hoping to catch a glimpse of her. And when I did see her, she was always veiled—and even then I was overwhelmed by her sight.

My main fear is that someone will come and take her away from me. Whenever I think of this possibility, I go mad with worry. Of all the maidens in the world, I want her as my lady. Let love be our guide. I used to be in love with JSDSQAQ, and no one else.[49] But now my affection for him and his family has increased for they have arranged for me to meet her, may the Lord reward them for this. Adieu, my beloved, until we are joined together in a few years.[50]

Thursday, May 13, 1915

In my great delight over yesterday's encounter I failed to write what I saw in the evening. After supper I walked back to my duties at the Commissariat. The road was crowded with soldiers, horses, carriages, and military supplies. I learned that orders had been given to the Tenth Battalion to relocate to the northern regions. The streets were pitch black, and I walked past the soldiers. Then

I came across the military band attached to the battalion, which was preparing to accompany them. All this movement brought joy to my heart, for it indicates that the government is in deep trouble. Just a few months ago the army was mobilizing to attack Egypt, but now that our English enemies are bombarding the cities from their fleet, the tables have turned. Istanbul is on the verge of collapse. Now they know that all their maneuvers are childish and that they are facing the most powerful adversaries on earth.

Jerusalem Municipality Expropriates Our Land
Thursday, May 13, 1915

Today we were informed that the Municipal Council was appropriating part of our family plot in Karm al A'raj to widen a public road.[51] I went there immediately and saw that the street had been widened by 8 *dra'* [yards]. What the council took from our plot would cost us at least 800 Ottoman pounds. Given the fact that the public treasury is more or less bankrupt, it is unlikely that we will see any compensation for this. I am not against the use of private property for public good, but the council should at least have taken into account our losses against the improvement in the value of land that our neighbors, the Quttaineh family, will now benefit from. At least it could have expropriated the land in a more equitable manner. Earlier this year it took another piece from our land worth about 200 pounds, which would add up to a loss of 1,000 pounds this year. If you add the 400 pounds my father paid in "war levies," it brings us to a total of 1,400 Ottoman pounds. I am still dependent on my family for support and will not see any property in my name as long as my father is alive, but I felt the losses as if they were my own.

At home in the evening, my father was philosophical about the whole affair. When I pressed him to appeal the decision, he became totally dismissive. "To whom should I complain?" he said. "You should not agitate yourself. At least we have our good health," he said.

Our Soldiers Stand Fast at Gallipoli
Friday, May 14, 1915

The Council of Learned Sheikhs [in Istanbul] issued a fatwa a few days ago bestowing the title al Ghazi [the Conqueror] to Sultan Muhammad Rashad V, in recognition of the victories achieved by our soldiers in this war, and particularly for the valor of our armed forces in Janaq Qal'a. I laughed when I read this news and said to myself, "Have they no shame?"

In the afternoon I went to check again on the area that the authorities were planning to confiscate. While there I met Master Khalil Effendi, and he noticed how upset I was. He too urged me to have my father file a complaint. I said, "How can we complain when our adversary is the government?" We walked together to Jaffa Gate. Before I left him, he asked me if I intend to go back to college after the war. I told him that yes, by all means I intend to go, unless—God forbid—the worst happens. We separated and went home.

I spoke with my father and suggested that he take my uncle Abu Rashid and pay a visit to Mayor Hussein Salim Effendi [al Husseini] to complain. I found that my father had already visited the mayor on his own. The mayor inquired and found out that the road scheme was wider than necessary, so he ordered a 2-meter reduction in the size of the expropriated land.

Today's Friday sermon in the Haram was by Sheikh As'ad

Shuqairi, the [parliamentary] deputy from Akka. It was mainly an admonition to the soldiers about desertion.[52]

Is Adel Effendi an Ottoman Spy?
Saturday, May 15, 1915

Agency reports arrived indicating that Asitanah [High Porte in Istanbul] is in great danger. Close to 180,000 enemy soldiers have landed and are surrounding the city. Yesterday news also reached us that 60 carriers have passed the Suez Canal loaded with soldiers and ammunition on the way to the Straits.[53] I was also told that Enver [Pasha] was killed.[54] May God make it true. American papers have reported that the English occupied Gallipoli on March 15 [Gregorian]. I am not sure about the credibility of this news.[55]

After supper I went to the house of Master Khalil [Sakakini] and met Hasan [Khalidi] there. We learned that Adel Jaber went early this morning to Jaffa on a mission for Cemal Pasha, accompanied by a man unknown to us. I have a suspicion that what Hasan said is probably true: Adel Effendi is a spy [for Cemal].[56]

Today a *firman* [imperial declaration] was announced for mobilizing people born in 1312 [1895].

Locust Swarms Reach Baq'a
May 20, 1915

Locust swarms are spreading everywhere, and the insects are laying their eggs. Crops have been laid waste across the country, but the situation is particularly severe around Jaffa and its environs. People arriving from the city report that citizens are compelled to go out in the fields and destroy the locusts. Those who refuse, or are unable to do so, are fined one Ottoman lira for each

Figure 12. Adel Jaber, teacher
at al-Salahiyya College and
opponent of Ihsan Turjman,
Jerusalem, 1915. Institute for
Palestine Studies, Beirut.

six days [of abstaining from collecting the insects]. I was told by
my mother that her brother saw the locust swarms in Baq'a.[57]
May God protect us.

Returning home this morning I passed a heavily equipped
battalion coming from Nablus. It was not clear whether it was on
its way to the Egyptian front or brought here to establish security.

I am completely in love, but I cannot talk to anybody about it,
although I have a feeling people around me know the situation.
She is the source of my happiness and misery at present. For I
am unable to marry her, knowing her father's opposition.[58] I go
to bed tonight with a heavy heart.

At the Military Hospital with Doctor Canaan
Sunday, May 23, 1915

I woke up today at 4:00 A.M. and went to the toilet with a heavy case of diarrhea. I returned to sleep and was woken again by the need to go the bathroom. At the Commissariat I took a referral to the military hospital for treatment. I found my cousin Hasan, who had been appointed as an assistant to Dr. [Tawfiq] Canaan.[59] Dr. Canaan examined me and gave me syrup and another stomach treatment. He gave me a two-day leave from service and advised me to come back to him if I do not see an improvement after I have completed the course of treatment.

At the Commissariat my officer saw the request for leave but refused to dismiss me until I finished a few tasks for him. I left in the afternoon and took the syrup, without having had any food yet. In the late afternoon I went to Jaffa Gate and found Taher Khalidi, and I ate four oranges he offered me, which I should have resisted. In the evening my cousin Hasan Effendi came to visit. He said that Italy has declared war on Austria, which means that Germany and our forces will also be involved. He was very optimistic and said that this development means that Rumania, Greece, and Bulgaria will now enter the war—which means that the war will be brought to a quick end.

We went to visit the professor [Sakakini] and discussed this subject. I went back late at night and found my mother still awake. We sat down and discussed the question of polygamy. She brought up the example set by the Prophet. My view was that he practiced polygamy as a way to bring together various groups and consolidate their alliance. We also discussed the Prophet's promoting the status of women in Islam and the example of the

Figure 13. Doctor Tawfiq Canaan (left), head of the Ottoman Military Hospital in Jerusalem, 1916. He treated Ihsan for the "frankish disease." Courtesy Library of Congress, Eric Matson Collection.

Ethiopian wife he brought from Abyssinia to Medina. I went to sleep at 12:30 A.M.

Typhus Is Spreading in Jerusalem
Monday, May 24, 1915

I was shocked to hear today about the death of Ahmad Effendi Nashashibi, the son of Haj Rashid Effendi and the brother of Ragheb Bey, the current deputy from Jerusalem. He died from typhus in the prime of his youth. He was buried this afternoon.[60]

Diseases are spreading like wildfire among the population, especially among Muslims—for they do not take the proper precautions, may God forgive us. I was told from one of the health inspectors in town that four typhus cases were reported in one day alone in Bab Hutta. When I heard the news, I was struck with great dread, not only for the people but also for myself. First, because I live and breathe all day among soldiers, in a place that is full of bugs and lice; and second, because of the lack of good hygiene in the workplace. Even though our home is one of the cleanest places, the roads and the entry to our neighborhood are among the filthiest places. I love life and enjoy its offerings. Please God, I am still very young, do not take me away.

Muhyi ed-Din Takes My Place at the Front
Tuesday, May 25, 1915

As I was passing by the Haram today on my way to work, I heard someone call my name. It was Sheikh Hadi Danaf, who informed me that my maternal cousin Muhyi ed-Din Effendi had arrived from Khan Yunis. My affection for Muhyi has no bounds, for he is my soul brother. At the beginning of the war I was stationed in Khan Yunis, and he was stationed at the Bireh garrison. He volunteered to replace me, and I was then sent to Bireh, and he went to the front in my place.

We had not received a letter from him for more than a month, which was a source of worry to all of us. I was feeling very guilty for taking his place.

I went immediately to his family home and received him with hugs and kisses. I had thought I would never see him again. His commanding officer was with him, an older man of about 65 who was released from service for his ill health. He told me that he will do his best to have Muhyi reassigned to Jerusalem, as a reward for his valor.

Later I reported to work, since my sick leave has expired. I had intended to ask permission to go to hospital to see the doctor again because my suffering [diarrhea] has not gone, but when I noticed that my officer was in a foul mood, I changed my mind.

Later in the evening I went to see Muhyi again, and he told me about his life in Khan Yunis. When he arrived, his officer asked him to compose a telegraph in Turkish, which he was unable to do. When the officers found out that he could write in Arabic, the commander of the Engineering Corps insisted that he be transferred to his division. One evening the commanding officer became very sick, and Muhyi served him and nursed him until he got better, so he became attached to him. Muhyi went twice to 'Arish to bring armaments. He suffered a great deal from the lack of food and water, but he continued to nurse the officer.

He told me that the locusts had invaded that area and consumed all the crops and tree leaves. Nothing was spared. English airplanes raided them on a daily basis, often dropping leaflets against the army and government. . . . [61]

Executions and Life Sentences
for Syrian and Palestinian Patriots
Thursday, September 1, 1915

A few years ago enlightened elements in the Syrian nation petitioned the Ottoman government in Beirut to implement basic reforms.[62] At the time intellectuals from Syria and Palestine, together with some notables from neighboring Arab countries, formed a movement based in Egypt and sent a delegation to Paris, where they met with leading French politicians to discuss their demands.[63] When the coalition government was formed, their voices were repressed, but that did not stop them. When the general mobilization was announced last year [1914], they went on the offensive and resumed their activities both openly and through clandestine groups.[64] The government, knowing their objectives, began to monitor their activities and employed a number of immoral agents to pursue them. It was able to intercept their correspondence, which included names of people that the state was unaware of. A large number of activists were arrested and were sent to the military tribunal in Sofar.[65] Many were sentenced to death, and others were given life sentences. Others were condemned to death in absentia.

Eleven were sentenced to death, including some of the best of our youth, such as Abdul Karim Effendi Khalil and the brothers Muhammad and Mahmoud Mahmassani. Also condemned to death were Hafiz Bey Said, the former parliamentary deputy from Jerusalem, as well as the mufti of Gaza. Because of the latters' learned status and their age, our lord the sultan commuted their sentence to life imprisonment. Similarly Rida Beyk Solh, former deputy from Beirut, and his son received life sentences.[66] Around 60 people were sentenced to death in absentia—including Rafiq Bey and Haqqi Bey Adhm [from Damascus] and Abdul Ghani Araysi, editor of *al Mufid* newspaper in Beirut. Also condemned to death were Doctor Shibly Shmayyel and Faris Nimr, owners of *al Muqattam* and *al Muqtataf*, as well as Sheikh Rashid Effendi Rida, editor of the Islamic journal *al Manar*, all published in Cairo.[67] The group included a writer from *al Ahram* and several others whose names I cannot remember.

I do not know any of these patriots, but I was deeply shaken by this news. Farewell to you, brave compatriots. May our souls meet when your noble objectives are realized.

We received news today that the British and French fleets are encircling Izmir and that some English soldiers have already landed in the city. News arrived also indicating that 300,000 British soldiers have been brought in to the Mediterranean. News from Janaq Qal'a indicates that there have been major Ottoman victories and that a large number of Entente soldiers have been killed or taken into captivity—but it is hard to verify the truthfulness of these numbers.

I Am Ottoman by Name Only, the World Is My Country
Friday, September 10, 1915

[Cemal Pasha] issued an order, communicated by phone to the Commissariat Wednesday evening at 5:30 P.M. It became known to him that many of those employed in the department of censorship, as well as the local police force and gendarmes, had been recruited from the local population. He therefore ordered that no members in the armed forces be allowed to serve in their [home] regions. Those serving will now be recorded in a special registry and transferred to the Beersheba Commissariat, where they will be dispatched away from their districts. Exception will be made for those in the fighting battalions *[tawabeer]*. Officers who violate this order will be subject to court-martial. This order was circulated within all sections of the Eighth Army here, to the offices of the Fourth and Eighth Armies in Damascus, and to all the military commissariats under Cemal Pasha's jurisdiction. The order requests the names of all soldiers in Jerusalem and its rural districts. The deadline for execution is the first of September (Ottoman calendar).

This circular led to a general panic in our area. Officers and soldiers began to seek all sorts of medical excuses to remain in Jerusalem.

The head of our Commissariat [Ruşen Bey] became very upset, since he did not want to lose his local staff, to whom he has become very attached, and because he knew that public works *[a'malkhana]* will be paralyzed in his region, since the majority of personnel come from the Jerusalem area. I heard the news within fifteen minutes of its arrival. Many of us were hoping that it would not be carried out. I was at a loss about what to do. I have too much dignity to plead exemption for myself, for I prefer to go to the front than to beg for mercy.

However, I cannot imagine myself fighting in the desert front. And why should I go? To fight for my country? *I am Ottoman by name only, for my country is the whole of humanity.*[68] Even if I am told that by going to fight, we will conquer Egypt, I will refuse to go. What does this barbaric state want from us? To liberate Egypt on our backs? Our leaders promised us and other fellow Arabs that we would be partners in this government and that they seek to advance the interests and conditions of the Arab nation. But what have we actually seen from these promises? Had they treated us as equals, I would not hesitate to give my blood and my life—but as things stand, I hold a drop of my blood to be more precious than the entire Turkish state.

If I go to the front, what will happen to my father and mother, and my siblings? When my parents heard of this circular, they started worrying about my fate even before any actual steps were taken. For they were already in great distress about the conditions at the war front and the miserable lot of our compatriots fighting there.

Will I Be Sent to the Front?
Wednesday, September 15, 1915

Several days have passed since Cemal Pasha issued his order, and nothing has happened. Many people here were hoping that it would be forgotten, even though in my heart of hearts I knew that I was destined to be sent to the front. This morning an order came from the Fourth Army HQ by telephone indicating that exception would be made for essential staff if their absence would affect the administration of the army. All others must be transferred.

In the evening the list of local soldiers was delivered to the commander of the Commissariat, from which he was to choose the names of those who could remain in the city. My officer went to see the commander and came back with the names of three soldiers who have to be sent to the front immediately. He mentioned the name of Taher Effendi Khalidi, but then he crossed out his name and inserted another in its place. Then he paused, remembering that I am also a Jerusalemite, and said that the final decision is in the hands of Ruşen Bey. I was too proud to ask him if my name was on the list. I knew that he had a great deal of affection toward me and that he would try to have me exempted, but I did not want to beg. When Taher arrived, I told him that his name was on the original list. He trembled, and his face lost its color. He said that he would go see his relative Hussein Effendi Salim Husseini [the deposed mayor] to ask him to intercede with Ruşen Bey. He then asked me about my intentions.

I said that I would follow the orders. He inquired if I wanted him to intercede on my behalf with Ruşen. I did not object, nor did I show much enthusiasm, for I would rather die than beg for his intercession. Deep in my heart I knew that my father would intercede, as he did at the beginning of the war when I was sent to the desert front via Hebron and he arranged for me to be transferred back to the city.

Today was the last day for the German ultimatum to Romania. The Germans had requested that their armies be allowed to cross Romanian territories on their way to Anatolia and then to the Egyptian front. Their aim, it seems, was to break the English-French stranglehold at Gallipoli, but it is not clear if Romania would allow them to do that.

Suicide Will Release Me from This Predicament
Tuesday, September 21, 1915

Today news arrived of the German ultimatum to Romania, in which Germany demanded that its armed forces be given right of entry into Romanian territory to march on Russia. The Romanians apparently are leaning toward accepting these conditions, but this report has not been verified yet. I am sick and tired of military life. I have no time nor possibility to do my reading. I leave home for HQ at 8:30 A.M. One hour for lunch at noon, and then I work at the Commissariat until 6:00 P.M. I take a short break for supper and then go back for a third time at 8:00 P.M. Most days we do not leave until 11:00. I usually go to bed at midnight. Whenever I take a book to work at HQ, my commanding officer expresses disgust with me. I am always on the lookout for someone approaching so that I can hide it. Also my fellow soldiers and officers are so rowdy that one can hardly concentrate.

I have seriously considered committing suicide as a way out of this trap, but I have changed my mind for one important reason. I do not want to make those who love me unhappy. Sooner or later this war will come to an end, but when . . . [line crossed out and unreadable]. After the end of the war, I will go to college for two years, study agriculture, and travel in Europe. If that does not work, I will study commerce and get married to my beloved. That is all I ask for. . . . I want to live by the sweat of my brow. If God chooses to bless me, I would like to have one or two children, to whom I will devote myself.

Ihsan's Dreams
Jerusalem, Wednesday, September 22, 1915[69]

Today I began taking private lessons in French. At the end of the war, I intend to attend college in Beirut. There I hope to perfect my French, reading, and writing. Then I will seek my family's approval to study agriculture in Switzerland.[70] Then I will come back, buy a piece of land to cultivate, and live with my beloved away from the crowds. Farming is the best profession, for if we look at all other crafts, we can find nothing nobler. My problem is that I have no command of French, and my family probably will not approve my travel to Europe.

Ruşen Bey Intercedes to
Block My Transfer to the Front
Thursday, September 23, 1915

An order was received at HQ listing the names of Jerusalem soldiers for transfer to the front. When the clerk read it, he became despondent, and so did several officers. I was to be stationed in

Dhaheriyyeh, which is seven hours away [from Jerusalem].[71] All the clerks in the room pressed him to do something about my name. He eventually went to the office of the chief of staff and was told that the presiding officer *[qomindan qarar-kah]* said that he does not need me in Jerusalem. Then he appealed the decision to Ruşen Bey, who decided to delete my name. The clerk then came and told me the good news. I thanked him profusely. I will never forget this favor. I would like to give him a gift, but it is too risky.[72]

The Syrians and Palestinians
Are a Cowardly and Submissive People
Thursday, September 30, 1915

Every major town in Syria and Palestine is sending a delegate to Janaq Qal'a to salute the memory of our martyrs in this war and to visit the wounded and inspire *[yahithu]* the living to continue with their jihad. The delegates from Jerusalem are Sheikh Taher Effendi Abul Su'ud, mufti of the Shafi'ies, and Sheikh Ali Effendi Rimawi. They left for Istanbul a few days ago.

This is a strange government. What do our leaders intend to accomplish with these games? Do they mean to strengthen the relationship between the Arab and Turkish nations *[umma]*? Or do they mean to incite religious fervor? Or perhaps they mean to satisfy the egos of religious clerics. What is definite is that the people are very unhappy with this government, but truth be told, the Palestinian and Syrian people *[sha'b]* are a cowardly and submissive lot. For if they were not so servile, they would have revolted against these Turkish barbarians.

The city crier *[munadi]* announced today that Ahmad Cemal Pasha, commander of the Fourth Army and minister of the navy, will sit every Friday in the Shari'a court to listen to petitions and complaints *[da'awi]* from the public. Agency news arrived today indicating that German troops have retreated from opposition in France. This could mean the beginning of defeat for the Austrians and the Germans. Thank God. We all need this war to come to an end. I do not care who wins and who loses. If this were a decent government that treats us properly, then my life and my companions' lives would be devoted to the nation. But, as it is, a drop of my blood (and a hair from my leg) is worth the thrones of the Ottoman sultans.

My Encounter with the Frankish Disease
Friday, October 8, 1915

While I was working in the Commissariat Tuesday evening, I felt a rash in my private parts. I thought it was some kind of blockage in my urinary tract. When I went home after 11:00 P.M. and urinated, I became alarmed by a white sticky substance that I was emitting. I became worried that it could be the sign of a venereal disease *[ta'qeebah]*, but how could I contract such a problem when I had no contact with anybody likely to be a source of the Frankish disease *[al da' al ifranji]*? God forbid. Yesterday I found two small pimples at the bottom of my rod. Finally on Thursday I went to see Hussein Effendi Khalidi, and I told him about my condition.[73] He immediately scared me by claiming that it is a venereal problem. I insisted that he give me some medicine, so he gave me a syrup to drink and warned me that my urine would turn blue upon use. Today I felt much better, so I went to thank him, but told him that I still have a burning sensation when I urinate. He told me not to worry and that the burning will disappear. When I asked him to explain what is happening to me, he began to interrogate me. I insisted that I haven't had any contact and finally convinced him. He said it probably happens because I play with it all the time. But I never do. Perhaps at night when I am asleep.

During all this period I was in a total panic. How could I contract a venereal disease when I had no contacts? Then I thought that perhaps I got it from associating [mu'ashara] with soldiers.[74] For three days I couldn't sleep, not knowing what to do. Thank God for removing this calamity.

If I had contracted the disease, what would I have done? I probably would have killed myself, since I would have made life miserable for my family, but also because I want to get married to my beloved T. and I do not want to ruin her life. Blessed I am, and blessed is Thurayya for a happy ending. Thank God, thank God, thank God.

Farewell, My Beloved Thurayya
Sunday, October 10, 1910

Here is a list of conditions for achieving happiness:

1. Once this war is over, I will study French and go to college in Beirut and finish my university education. Better still to study agriculture in Europe.

2. I will marry Thurayya, which is my secret name for her.[75] My love for her is limitless, especially now that I have seen her face without cover.

I know that Thurayya is rather ignorant in matters pertaining to the management of the household, but living with her will overcome this liability.[76] This lady is one of the most refined and educated women in Jerusalem and Palestine. How happy I will be to be her partner. But I cannot marry her for three or four years—at best. My fear is that someone will take her before I do.

What gives me hope is a story that I heard about the time when her family was approached by a Jerusalemite [for her hand], and her family declined. A lady gossiper who was visiting at the time reproached her mother: Do you really want her to marry so and so, where she will live in a household that has no master? Her mother rebuked the woman and asked her not to interfere. Clearly they know about my intentions.

Farewell, Thurayya. Farewell, my beloved. I think only of you.

Ahmad Cemal Pasha Is Transferred to Aleppo with the Fourth Army
Saturday, October 20, 1915

For three days I have been suffering from yellow fever. I am in a state of perpetual fatigue. On Tuesday after I had lunch with my family, I went to my room, where I fell on the floor. I went to see Dr. Canaan, who gave me some treatment. Hussein, my cousin, insists that this fatigue is caused by a liver disease.

Very little news from agency reports. The field of operations seems to have moved from Europe to the Balkans. Greece is still neutral, but it seems that the present prime minister will resign and will be succeeded by the famous nationalist Venizelos, who is known for being pro-war.[77] The railroad line connecting us to Beersheba has been strafed by enemy [British] planes. A month ago Ahmad Cemal Pasha left for Aleppo with most of his staff. His reasons are unknown but suspect, especially now that the promised invasion of Egypt is imminent.

A few days ago I went to the German Military Command in Jerusalem (housed where the German post office used to be) to

look at illustrated clippings from the war. Here they have articles and pictures clipped from Arabic, Turkish, German, and
French journals, basically aimed at winning people for the war
effort—but nobody here trusts this propaganda. In *Servet i Funun*
[The Wealth of Knowledge], the renowned Turkish journal published in Istanbul, I saw a picture of an English banknote found
with a captured British soldier, which was embossed in both
Turkish and English. Probably the English are so sure of captur-
ing Istanbul that they are preparing themselves.

People are dying of hunger. All essential foodstuffs are missing,
including material produced in other Ottoman provinces. Citizens can no longer bear this situation. A pound *[ratl]* of flour costs
8 piasters.[78] And this is from locally grown wheat. You can imagine the cost of buying imported sugar, where a pound of sugar
costs 60 piasters (Jerusalem mint). Rice is 30 piasters (1.5 majidi).[79]

Many of the soldiers destined for the Egyptian campaign have
arrived in our region and will be entering Jerusalem in the next
few days. May God protect them and return them home safely.

Attack on Egypt Postponed
Thursday, October 25, 1915

An agency telegram was received today announcing a sultanic
decree promoting Fourth Army Commander Ahmad Cemal
Pasha to the rank of *fareeq* [vice admiral], as a reward for his services and military victories. Which victories is not clear. Certainly not the Egyptian campaign.

Rumors abound that Cemal Pasha is to be recalled to Istanbul
and that the Supreme Command in Turkey has decided against
a [second] Egyptian campaign this summer for the lack of military preparedness.

Diseases are taking their terrible toll in Aleppo and Homs. Sixty to seventy deaths a day, mostly Armenians.

Are We about to Have a Bread Rebellion?
Monday, December 17, 1915

I haven't seen darker days in my life. Flour and bread have basically disappeared since last Saturday. Many people have not eaten bread for days now. As I was going to the Commissariat this morning, I saw a throng of men, women, and boys fighting each other to buy flour near Damascus Gate. When I passed this place again in midday, their numbers had multiplied. Most of the newcomers were peasants. I became very depressed and said to myself, "Pity the poor"—and then I said, "No, pity all of us, for we are all poor nowadays."

Two days ago we ran out of flour at home, and we had nothing to eat. My father gave my brother Aref a few pennies to buy us bread.[80] He looked everywhere, but there was no bread to be bought anywhere. One of our cousins sent us a bag of semolina *[smeed]* when he heard of our distress. Yesterday my grandmother's sister Um Ibrahim also sent us three pounds of flour. Without this help we would have gone hungry.

I never thought we would lack flour in our country, when we are the source of wheat. And I never in my life imagined that we would run out of flour at home. Who is responsible but this wretched government? It tried to establish a pricing regime *(fi'a)* for wheat and flour—which was a good idea—but it should have established means for the delivery of flour before establishing the rations. What will happen when [the merchants] refuse to sell? The rich in Jerusalem, as in other cities, have taken provisions and hoarded a year's supply in their cellars. But what can the poor do? If the government had any dignity, it would have saved wheat in its hangars for public distribution at a fixed price, or even have made it available from military supplies.

If these conditions persist, the people will rebel and bring down this government—and then it will be too late for the leaders to atone for their sins. We have so far tolerated living without rice, sugar, and kerosene. But how can we live without bread? Beginning with the new month [Ottoman calendar], the price conversions have been fixed as follows:

New Currency	Old Currency
gurush	*gurush*
120 per English pound	136.10 per English pound
108 per Ottoman lira	125.10 per Ottoman lira
95 per French pound	109 per French pound
20 per majidi	23 per majidi
One qirsh is worth	
3 matleeks, and 2.5 paras	xxxxxxxx

Today Is My Birthday
Thursday, December 20, 1915[81]

On my way to the Commissariat today I saw the police forcing shopkeepers to hang and raise flags in celebration of a public holiday. But which holiday? The sultan's birthday? Or the anniversary of annulling the Capitulations?[82] The occasion turned out to be the founding of the Ottoman dynasty by Sultan Uthman I.

The appointment of a new commander for the First Egyptian Campaign, the German General von Kressennstein, was announced today.[83] Our master, Cemal the Great, is now a mere vice

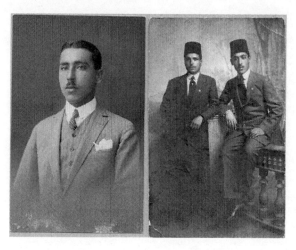

Figure 14. Ihsan Turjman on his twenty-third birthday (left), with unidentified friend, Jerusalem, 1916. Courtesy Turjman family.

admiral—but he will continue to command the Fourth Army. The title Commander of the First Egyptian Campaign must have been created to avoid confusion, since he will be serving formally under Cemal's command—but only formally. But why "First" Campaign? Forgive me—I forgot the previous campaign was only exploratory. I was told by a government supporter today that German officers have begun to arrive here [Jerusalem] in large numbers.

Writing in Code
Saturday, January 2, 1916

The Camel Corps [Hajjanah] arrived in Jerusalem yesterday—no fewer than 500 soldiers. Last week another two battalions arrived. I heard that those are mostly tribesmen from Medina [in Hijaz] who volunteered to fight the English for a steady monthly salary of 5 Ottoman pounds. The huge number of soldiers in the city indicates that a decision has been taken to resume the attack on the [Suez] Canal. I think we will face another defeat—for who can believe that we can defeat the British fleet and the English army and continue to take over Egypt? But maybe I am totally ignorant.

Sunday [no date]

[in code] *I never heard such harsh words from him before. He kept telling me that I do not do what he asks me to do. I was despondent all day.*

The financial crisis is getting worse every day. May God have mercy on us.

[in code] *As I was writing in my diary today, my father called me. I went over, thinking it was an urgent matter. He said, "I am fed up. Your mother is a spendthrift, always giving away cigarettes to the guests." Then he started shouting. What a shame. He is getting senile. Cannot blame him. I went to my mother and told her the story.*

Yesterday, Saturday, I thought of using a numerical code for writing. I used it for five minutes, got bored, and left it. Today I used it for ten minutes. I also kept the code key on a separate paper. It really is very easy.

*Ottoman Victories in Dardanelles:
Haifa and Jaffa Bombarded from the Sea*

Monday, January 10, 1916

Last evening a telegraph was received [by the Commissariat] from Cemal Pasha, commander of the Fourth Army indicating that our English and French enemies have retreated toward the south. All departments were to take the day off in celebration today, Monday. Sweets are to be distributed to all soldiers. All shops and public places are to be lit—except for coastal facilities [which have to stay on alert]. I said to myself, "Every time we celebrate a victory we face a disaster a few days later."

I had hardly recorded that thought when news arrived of the following: battleships arrived in Haifa few days ago and bombarded the German Colony.[84] The whole neighborhood was deserted. A friend of mine reported also from the Eighth Army that Jaffa was bombarded. We were told that HQ would send the 27th Division (the Jerusalem Battalion, *firqa*). I said to myself, "What can the Jerusalem Battalion do in the face of coastal bombardment?" A few days ago an ammunition dump blew up in Afula. It contained 48 boxes of dynamite. Scores of soldiers died, and the explosion could be heard from Haifa.

A Popular Reception for Enver Pasha, Minister of War
Tuesday, February 29, 1916

Ten days ago we were given notice of the imminent arrival of Enver Pasha, minister of war, to be accompanied by Minister of the Navy and Commander of the Fourth Army Ahmad Cemal Pasha and senior officers from the Ottoman, Austrian, and German general staffs. Today they finally arrived. City shops were closed, and the streets were decorated with arches of triumph. Everybody went to Jaffa Road to meet the entourage. At 5:15 P.M. the motorized procession arrived at Sheikh Bader, where the official reception took place. After the group had some refreshments, the fleet of cars moved to the Mount of Olives *[et-Tur]*. Students, men, and women, as well as dignitaries and clerics from all religious groups, were lined up all the way up and

down both sides of the street to greet the leader of the Turkish nation.

The second day Enver visited the Holy Sanctuary and al-
Salahiyya College, as well as various historical sites.[85] He and
his companions were feasted at Fast Hotel hosted by the municipality [of Jerusalem]. Sunday morning he went to Beersheba and
the desert [fronts], and was back by 2:30 P.M. Dinner was served
in the Commissariat that evening. Sheikh As'ad Effendi Shuqairi
gave a speech during the banquet and proposed that Enver Pasha
establish a library in Jerusalem to immortalize his name on the
occasion of this visit.[86] At 10:30 everybody was gone. This great
leader will now depart to Medina with Ahmad Cemal to visit the
tomb of the Prophet [al Mustafa] via Jericho, Salt, and Ma'an.[87]
The group was accompanied by the mufti of Jerusalem.[88] His
Excellency Enver Pasha donated over 500 Ottoman liras to the
poor and made several other offerings, may God reward him and
protect him.

Our House Is Robbed, Thieves Arrested
Friday, April 14, 1916

On Saturday, the 8th of April, I quit smoking. This is how it
happened. I was headed home from my work at the Commissariat accompanied by my neighbor and friend the pharmacist
from Nablus, Rustum Effendi Abu Ghazaleh. We agreed to stop
smoking due to the difficulty we were both encountering in finding tobacco. It's been a week now, and I hope not to smoke again
as long as this war continues. If peace is concluded, I might go
back to smoking. It seems, however, that my friend [Rustum] has
gone back to smoking.

We had a house outside the wall opposite Damascus Gate.

Last year we leased it to Hikmat Effendi, a justice of the peace in the local court. This year he left the house, and the place became vacant. When we heard that the government intended to seize all unoccupied apartments, our family moved in there and we lived in it for a whole month. During this period our home in the old city was robbed. Here are the details: On Friday, February 11th, my father needed some items from the old house, so he sent my [younger] brother Aref. When Aref entered the house, he realized immediately that the place had been robbed and came running back to tell us. My father, mother, and uncle hurriedly went over there. My sister Asma was sent to fetch me. Here is a preliminary list of the stolen items:

- Fur coat belonging to my late aunt Safiyya
- Two gold watches
- Prayer beads made of amber
- Two or three pieces of women's jewelry
- Four silver spoons—gold plated
- An earring
- A ring (left for safekeeping)
- A box of jewelry belonging to my aunts, contents unknown.

It is likely that more that one thief was involved. The intruder had broken an iron-framed window in the western wall and entered at night. A kerosene lamp and candle residue were found on the floor. From the manner of theft, it seemed that the robber or robbers intended to come back because the house was empty. What upset us more than the robbery was the fact that the thieves had pissed on the floor during their entry. Initially we had no idea who did it. A day later, it transpired that it was Ahed Danaf and his accomplices. What made us suspect him was that on the morning of the robbery [Friday], he had seen my sister Yusra in the street and asked her if we intended to return home to sleep that evening and wanted to know what our plans were, etc.

We filed a complaint with the police against him. He was arrested, interrogated, and then released on bond *[tahta al kafalah]*. A few days later he was conscripted and sent to the front. The issue sort of died.

On Friday, April 13th, my father received an unsigned letter, which Aref found in a niche at the entrance to the house, indicating that the unknown writer had seen Abdul Salam Abul Sa'ud, my maternal cousin, and Abdul Afu Danaf, son of Sheikh Said Danaf, at a goldsmith's shop (with his name stated). The men had a small bag containing the golden watches, which they wanted to have melted down and made into golden rings.

My brother Aref went immediately to the jeweler's shop accompanied by Omar Danaf (son of Sheikh Amin). He questioned the jeweler until he admitted that the incident had taken place. My father then took all these details to the police. Three days later, as it happened, my cousin, Abdul Salam Abul Sa'ud, was conscripted and taken to Damascus. A few days later this ill-fated *[manhus]* lad returned to Jerusalem with a month's leave from service since he belonged to the 1313 birth cohort. The arrest papers kept moving from one government department to another until they reached the offices of the military tribunal *[al diwan al 'urfi]*. By that time the stolen items had been hurriedly sold to a pawnbroker. Yesterday I went with Ahmad Effendi Ja'uni to the house of the pawnbroker, who panicked and confirmed that he had bought the stolen items. He showed us the fur coat, the spoons, the amber beads, and the golden earrings. He said he had sold one of the watches. Abdul Salam was immediately arrested, as well as Abdul Afu. Investigations continue.

The Court Passes Sentence
April 25, 1916

During lunch today my brother Aref told me that he went to the military tribunal to testify on behalf of my father about the robbery complaint. The [the investigators] asked him several questions, which he answered; then he added on his own that I [Ihsan] had heard that my cousin Abdul Salam had given the gold watch to Ali Taftaf, who in turn passed it to Mann so that suspicions would fall on him alone. I heard this story from Sheikh Huda Danaf when I saw him last week. I became very upset with Aref—first, because I hate to appear in court, and second, because the case is against my own cousin.

At 2 P.M. my commanding officer at the Commissariat told me that I had been summoned to appear at the military tribunal. I went there immediately, where they kept me waiting till 3:30. I was then called into court, together with my cousin Abdul Salam, Mann, and Ali Taftaf. The courtroom was medium size. The trial committee was made up of a lieutenant *[beykbashi]*, a sergeant *[qulghasi]*, a public prosecutor, and the clerk, who was my uncle Aziz Effendi Daudi.[89]

This was the first time I had ever appeared in a court. How horrible it was: I trembled with every word I uttered. My voice failed me several times during the testimony.

After giving my name, age, and profession, I was asked to narrate the story of the robbery. I gave all the details briefly. Then they [the court investigators] asked me if I knew the accused—my cousin Abdul Salam, Ishaq Mann, and Ali Taftaf. I said yes. Then they asked me if I believed that they are the robbers. I said that I could say only that it appears from the unsigned letter that they are the thieves.

Figure 15. Ottoman prison known as Habs al Damm, African Quarter, Jerusalem, 1901. Courtesy Library of Congress, Eric Matson Collection.

The three accused men denied everything initially. Later when the lieutenant attacked Mann and Abdul Salam, they admitted their deed. They and Ahed Danaf. Ali Taftaf insisted that he wasn't with them and had nothing to do with it.

Initially Mann said repeatedly that Taftaf was their accomplice, obviously because he wanted to entrap him into the affair, since he was his companion. But after he was beaten, he confessed that Taftaf was not in their company. Which was the truth, because I knew Ali Taftaf was very sick the day of the robbery, and I told this to the court.

I was later told that the military tribunal gave prison terms to Ahed Danaf, Abdul Salam Abul Sa'ud, and Ishaq Mann. Each one of them was also to pay a fine of two and a half pounds.

My Father Refuses to Drop Charges

Here I must say this for the record. When I found out that my cousin was the robber, I immediately started working to have this case dismissed, before it reached the courts. I found it difficult to convince my father, since he was so agitated by the case. My father knew of my intentions. I tried to prevail on him to withdraw the case as a favor to my mother and to my sisters and brothers.

[in code] *God forgive him. He wanted to punish my* [maternal aunt]. *She was having dinner with us only ten days ago. Is there any self-respect in his attitude? Isn't it a shame that he does this? The honorable thing to do here was to show a measure of magnanimity and forgive my cousin.*

Why can't he forgive my cousin, who is only a boy of 17 years? What does he hope to achieve by pursuing this case? I can only surmise here that he is being vindictive.

Now the ill-fated boy has been sentenced to two years [imprisonment]. What will happen to him? What can he do? His mother is too poor to take care of him. His uncles do not give a damn about him. If he dies of want, the fate of this miserable boy will be of our doing.

Defeated British Soldiers Brought to Jerusalem
Tuesday, May 9, 1916

On May ... [date missing] about 70 injured Ottoman soldiers arrived. On the 15th of May, Friday afternoon, English prisoners arrived in the city.[90] They included one general *[miralai]*, one lieutenant, and about 20 officers of various ranks. The rest were 250 soldiers—English, Indian, Irish, etc. . . . At 12:30 the prisoners arrived by rail in Jerusalem station, guarded by Turkish soldiers. All officers arrived in the velvet [first-class] compartments. In front was the English general, sitting next to the Ottoman commander. He had a lot of dignity and defiance but was obviously despondent and angry. The rest of the officers seemed less concerned with their fate and displayed a carefree attitude, as is customary among the English. All prisoners were wearing their uniforms except two, who arrived wearing flannels. I was told that they were taken prisoners in a surprise raid near Beersheba. All officers were lodged in the hospital opposite the Commissariat (Notre Dame de France).[91] Soldiers were incarcerated in a bigger building nearby, on Soap Factory Road.

This is how these soldiers fell into captivity:

Last week preparations were under way for a major battle in the Beersheba area. One day before the encounter, one of our pilots made an exploratory trip over the British encampment. The next day at dawn, our soldiers moved to the encampment of the Fifth Army and surrounded the British camp while the soldiers were still asleep. They woke up in total panic. A short battle ensued in which—according to the official telegraph reports—four contingents were wiped out before they surrendered. Our losses were light. At this point British warplanes began to attack the site, which incurred considerable Ottoman losses. The Ottomans claim that the captured general is a leading commander in the British army, but who knows? How can he respect himself when he allowed himself and his battalion to be captured while asleep?

No Provisions in the City
Monday, July 10, 1916

I can hardly concentrate these days. We face both a general war and an internal war. The government is trying (with futility) to bring food supplies, and disease is everywhere. It's been over a month now since I have written anything in my diary.

Jerusalem has not seen worst days. Bread and flour supplies have almost totally dried up. Every day I pass the bakeries on my way to work, and I see a large number of women going home empty-handed. For several days the municipality distributed some kind of black bread to the poor, the likes of which I have never seen. People used to fight over the limited supplies, sometimes waiting in line until midnight. Now, even that bread is no longer available.

Banknotes. New banknotes were issued in the value of 20 and 25 Ottoman liras. They are guaranteed by the "Administration of Public Debts." I have no idea what these public debts are. Are these state debts to Austria and Germany? Where are the shares [owed by] France, England, and the other countries? Initially the government printed 5 and 1 lira notes. Almost immediately the value of the lira began to fall—from 102 qirsh [piasters] to the lira, down to 70, 68, 60, and now 58 qirsh to the lira. What is stranger is that many government departments do not accept payment of their own debts in paper currency.

All the prices have gone up, and very few items are available in the market. You cannot find lentils, onions, or any vegetables produced locally, yet quite a few imported items are still available. But who can buy them?

Sherif Hussein Declares Rebellion against the State
[same date]

Rebellion. Sherif Hussein Pasha declared rebellion against the state. There were demonstrations in Medina, and some of the Hijazi rail lines were destroyed. But the rebels' numbers were few, and they were dispersed.

Could this be the beginning? Every Arab should be pleased about this news.

How can we support this state after it killed our best youth? They were hanged in public squares like common criminals and gangsters. They were executed for demanding their rights and for questioning their fate in the general conscription. They died, and not one voice was raised in protest in this miserable Arab nation. Not one Palestinian or Syrian voice. May God bless our Hijazi leader and strengthen his hand.

Our government is doing its utmost to hide new of this [rebellion]. Secret police are everywhere to suppress it, but to no avail. News arrived indicating that the English have sent a large contingent of Indian and Egyptian soldiers to Hijaz and that Jeddah and Makka are in Arabian hands. The Arabians in Hijaz have now retreated, but not for long, may God support them.

Reasons for the Hijazi Sedition

Hijazi agitation is caused by several factors. Some say that Sherif Hussein Pasha made a special plea for clemency, seeking to get an annulment of the execution orders for the Arab leaders, but this was denied. Another reason is that the government used to make an annual payment to the Hijazi tribes to compensate them for the losses they incurred when the Hijazi rail lines were built.[92]

Apparently this year Cemal Pasha, our great helmsman, decided not to pay this compensation. Hence the rebellion.

May God bless the sherif of Hijaz and strengthen his arm. And may your campaign spread to every corner of the Arab lands, until we get rid of this cursed state. When the barbaric Ottoman state executed the Arab leaders last year, and then again this year, not a word of protest was made. But now their moment [of retribution] has finally arrived.

The Albanian Officer Makes an Outrageous Gesture
Monday, August 17, 1916

They say that July is the best month of the year, since it witnessed the liberation of nations. For me it has been the ugliest and vilest of months. I have not seen more difficult days in my life. I have thought often of taking my life. I even have begun praying to God to take me away from this world, so that I will be freed from the miserable life of soldiering.

When I became depressed, I asked my pharmacist friend to give me a treatment to help me get discharged. I insisted, but he refused. I needed a medicine that would make me so sick that they would be compelled to give me a leave for few months. My life is very valuable, but my honor is more precious—for I would rather die than dishonor myself.

Here is what happened. On Friday, the first of July 1332, by the Eastern [Ottoman fiscal] calendar, as I was working at my desk at the Commissariat, my officer *[katibi]*, who is an Arna'uti,[93] asked me to read a paper on which he had written a few lines. Then he tore it into pieces before I could see it. I was confused about its contents, since it was not meant to be an official statement for the registry that I was filing. Minutes later he came over and said that he wanted to kiss me between the eyes. My face became pale, and I wanted to beat him up, but I decided to control myself and did not respond.

He came back and said he wanted an answer. "Do not fear," he said, "I do not want to harm you. I love you tremendously. God knows why, for I cannot bear this situation anymore, and I have been suffering [from your love] for over 20 days." I said nothing.

Then he asked me to allow my forehead and hair to show underneath my military cap. He dismissed me and allowed me to go home. I left in a delirium, unaware of my surroundings. What should I do now? Should I take my life? But I am very young, and I have a lot to live for. If I committed suicide, what would happen to my parents? I was tempted to report him to the commander, or to my uncle, but was too embarrassed to speak about this matter.

I ate very little that evening. I had no appetite but had to behave as if I were hungry since my family was fasting [Ramadan] and my father believed that I too was fasting. Several days passed, and the officer, God curse him, kept pursuing me. Every time we were alone, he suggested unspeakable things—sometimes approaching me in a pleasant manner and sometimes roughly. He was constantly trying to kiss me and asking me to show my hair. After five days of pursuit, he finally left me alone for a whole day. I was relieved for a short period.

The next day as I was going home after work, I saw my neighbor Rustum Effendi, the pharmacist, and walked with him toward Jaffa Gate. There I saw the [Albanian] officer, who called me and said, "I do not want to see you in the company of this man [Rustum] any time, day or night." Sparks came out of his eyes, and he came so close that I was certain he was going to hit me. I gathered my courage and told him that I could not go with him at that moment and asked him to pass by our house from the external side, since the Haram compound is closed at night, and our house is inside.[94] Then he dismissed me.

Several days have passed since I wrote the above. Every day since then he has been confronting me, God damn him. Sometimes he would say, "Get out of my way," which gave me a sense of relief. But then he would come back and say, "How can I leave you? I cannot bear to be away from you." And sometimes he would say, "I do not want to see you speaking to Hilmi Effendi Husseini or Rustum Effendi, the pharmacist." I often saw him at the café by Damascus Gate, or by its road, observing me and the company I keep.

He fought several times with Rustum Effendi, claiming that Rustum keeps me from doing my work and that he is harmful company. Many times he obstructed my path as I left work at night. He would threaten to kill me, or to kill himself. What sent terror into my heart was when I saw him one day writing on a piece of paper (I could not see what he wrote)—then he looked at me and said, "You will die from what is written here."

When the clerical sergeant was in his company, he would show his sweet side and treat me with kindness and praise me in front of him. But I do not care for his praise, nor for his sweetness, for I do not want to fall into the depravity he is leading me to.

This is my story in brief. But what will happen to me with this treacherous man?

An Annoying Visit after Midnight and
a Complaint to Ruşen Bey
Tuesday, August 8, 1916

My mother woke me up late at night. "Get up, your officer is waiting for you." "Where?" "He is downstairs in the Haram," she said. I put on my jacket and my cap and went to see him. He was sitting on the marble slab near our house by the southern side of al-Sultaniyyah. The doorman of the holy sanctuary was standing next to him. I asked him the purpose of his visit. He said he wanted three things from me. First, to have Rustum Effendi evicted from his house.[95] Second, to let my hair down so that is visible from my cap. Third, he wanted some papers that I had in fact delivered to him two days ago. He claimed that both Commander Ruşen Bey, inspector of the Commissariat, and Nihad Bey, the chief of staff, wanted these papers urgently.

I finally got rid of him. It was 1:30 past midnight, *franji* time. I returned home and found Rustum Effendi standing by the staircase eavesdropping on our conversation. I left him and told my parents that my officer wanted some papers urgently. I went to bed but could not sleep. For an hour and half I turned in my bed wondering what to do with this loathsome character. Finally I resolved to go first thing in the morning and discuss the whole issue with my uncle.

At 6:30 in the morning, *franji* time, I hurriedly ate my breakfast and went to see my uncle. I told him the whole story in full detail. He listened, then asked me to calm down, and promised that he would find a way to deal with it. I left him feeling much better and went straight to the Commissariat. I arrived there late and found [the Albanian officer] still in bad shape from yesterday's intoxication. He asked me if I spoke with anybody about the matter. I replied in the negative. He remained sick all day from his condition and did not eat a morsel.

In the evening I went to see my uncle and asked him if he had done anything. He said that he had found an interlocutor who promised to arrange a meeting with Commander Ruşen Bey, so that he can present a complaint to him. I asked him to delay the meeting since I felt that the Albanian was beginning to behave properly, and we may as well forget the whole issue

This bloody saga has been going on for some time. One moment he is kind and considerate, and I feel relieved, and the next thing he is back to his old habits. And then I say to myself, no, no, I cannot bear this anymore.

. . .

[The diary ends abruptly here. In testimony by Salih Turjman, the son of Ihsan's younger brother, he relates that his father, Adel Bey Turjman, told him prior to his death that Ihsan was murdered by an Ottoman officer before Allenby's army entered Jerusalem in the winter of 1917.]

I remember Aref and Adel Bey al-Turjman, and their good father, the honorable Hasan Bey. I keep asking forgiveness for their brother Ihsan, whose sweet memory never leaves my thoughts—May God have mercy on his soul.

Khalil Sakakini, Damascus Central Prison, July 11, 1918

NOTES

THE ERASURE OF OTTOMAN PALESTINE

Second epigraph: Quoted in an interview with Samir Awad, grandson of Umbashi Awad, July 16, 2006. Awad was from the village of Anabta, and he fought in Suez and Gallipoli.

1. For a good selection of World War I soldiers' diaries, see Edward Lengel's "In the Trenches: The Soldier's Experience in World War I," which provides an extensive network of diaries from several World War I sites: http://wsrv.clas.virginia.edu/~egl2r/wwi.html (accessed November 22, 2008). For Ottoman sources, see Altay Atli, Turkey in the First World War, http://www.turkeyswar.com/campaigns/palestine1 .htm (accessed December 9, 2009). This site has an extensive section on Palestine.

2. *Ashraf* were the potentates of the city, claiming lineage from the Prophet Muhammad.

3. John Gerber, "Anton Pannekoek and the Quest for an Emancipatory Socialism," *New Politics,* no. 5 (Summer 1988).

4. "The only war left for Prussia-Germany to wage will be a world war, a world war, moreover, of an extent and violence hitherto unimagined. Eight to ten million soldiers will be at each other's throats and in the process they will strip Europe barer than a swarm of locusts. The

depredations of the Thirty Years' War compressed into three to four years and extended over the entire continent; famine, disease, the universal lapse into barbarism, both of the armies and the people, in the wake of acute misery; irretrievable dislocation of our artificial system of trade, industry and credit, ending in universal bankruptcy; collapse of the old states and their conventional political wisdom to the point where crowns will roll into the gutters by the dozen and no one will be around to pick them up; the absolute impossibility of foreseeing how it will all end and who will emerge as victor from the battle. Only one consequence is absolutely certain: universal exhaustion and the creation of the conditions for the ultimate victory of the working class. That is the prospect for the moment when the systematic development of mutual one-upmanship in armaments reaches its climax and finally brings forth its inevitable fruits." Fredrick Engels, quoted by Gilbert Achcar in "Engels: Theorist of War, Theorist of Revolution," *International Socialism Journal*, no. 97: 38.

5. Khaled Fahmy, *All the Pasha's Men: Mehmed Ali, His Army, and the Making of Modern Egypt*, Cambridge Middle East Studies 8 (Cambridge: Cambridge University Press, 1997).

6. Salah Issa, *Rijal Raya wa Sekina: Sira Ijtima'yya wa Siyasiyya* (Cairo: Dar Al Ahmadi, 2002).

7. Ibid., 111–12.

8. Ibid.

9. For a history of these units, see Erik Jan Zürcher, "Ottoman Labour Battalions in World War I," Working Papers Archive, Department of Turkish Studies, Leiden University, March 2002.

10. Khalil Totah and Omar Salih Barghouti, *The History of Palestine* (Jerusalem: 1920), 248–52.

11. On the "recruitment" of the labor battalions, see ibid., 249; Khalil Sakakini, *Yawmiyyat, Rasa'il, Ta'amulat 1906–1948* [Khalil Sakakini, Diaries, Letters, Reflections 1906–1948], 8 vols. (Beirut: Institute for Palestine Studies, 2006–2010), hereafter, Sakakini diary; Ihsan Turjman, war diary, Jerusalem 1915–16, unpublished diary manuscript, hereafter, Turjman diary. All citations, including page numbers, derive from the Arabic published version of the diary: Salim Tamari, *'Am al Jarad: al*

Harb al Uthma wa Mahu al Madi al Uthmani fi Filastin (Beirut: Institute for Palestine Studies, 2008). All chapter headings and subheadings are mine, except for the one heading Turjman provided on his birthday. Diary translated by Salim Tamari.

12. Omar Salih Barghouti, *al-Marahil: Tarikh siyasi* [Turning Points: A Political History] (Beirut: al-Mu'assasa al-'Arabiyya li al-dirasat wa al-nashr, 2001), 192; and Jens Hanssen, "Public Morality and Marginality in *Fin-de-siècle* Beirut," in *Outside In: On the Margins of the Modern Middle East,* ed. Eugene Rogan (London: I. B. Tauris, 2002), 186–89.

13. Totah and Barghouti, *The History of Palestine,* 253–54.

14. The works of Aziz Duri, Philip Khoury, Adel Mana, Abdul Karim Rafiq, Dina Rizek, and Rashid Khalidi come to mind. See most recently Muhammad 'Afifi, *'Arab wa 'uthmaniyyun: ru'ya mughayira* (Cairo: Dar al-Shuruq, 2005).

15. Goncu quoted by Jonathan Gorvett, "The Forgotten Arabs of Gallipoli," *Al Jazira Net,* January 14, 2004, http://english.aljazeera.net/archive/2004/01/2008491351293268110.html (accessed October 2007).

16. Sellers quoted in ibid., 3–4.

17. Ihsan's exact birth date is unknown. I have calculated it from approximations of his schooling dates and the known birth dates of his brothers and sisters.

18. The information about Muhammad Fasih's family comes from the English edition of his diary, *Diary of Lt Mehmed Fasih 5th Imperial Ottoman Army, 1915,* trans. and ed. Hasan Basri Danisman (Istanbul: Denizler Kitabevi, 2003), henceforth Fasih, *Diary;* the original version was transliterated from Ottoman Turkish by Murat Çulcu (Istanbul: Arba, 1997). The information about the Turjman family comes from Ihsan's diary.

19. Mehmed Fasih, *Kanlısırt günlüğü : Mehmed Fasih Bey'in Çanakkale anıları/yay. haz. [i.e., yayına hazırlayan],* transliterated and edited by Murat Çulcu (Beyoğlu, İstanbul: Denizler Kitabevi, Kaptan Yayıncılık, 2002), 18–120.

20. Communication with Irvin Schick, Cambridge, June 16, 2009. I thank Professor Schick for his helpful comments on the Fasih diary.

21. Hasan Danisman, introduction to Fasih, *Diary,* viii.

22. Fasih, *Diary,* 136–39.

23. Danisman, epilogue to Fasih, *Diary,* 209.

24. Fasih, *Diary,* 61–62. Fasih uses the Turkish spelling of these Arab names.

25. Ibid., 74.

26. Ibid., 63. The mention of German officers refers to Germans seconded to the Ottoman army as advisors and trainers.

27. The history of this property is told in Thomas Abowd, "The Politics and Poetics of Place: The Baramki House," *Jerusalem Quarterly,* no. 21 (2004): 49–58.

28. *Yawmiyyat Muhammad al Salih min ahali al alquds, 1333 [1914–1915],* Manuscripts Department, AP.AR 846, National Library, Hebrew University, Jerusalem.

29. Mana's book was published by the Institute for Palestine Studies, Beirut.

30. Abigail Jacobson, "Negotiating Ottomanism in Times of War: Jerusalem during World War I Through the Eyes of a Local Muslim Resident," paper presented at the conference "The Roots of Liberal Thought in the Eastern Mediterranean," Erlangen, Germany, July 30-August 3, 2005. I am very grateful to Dr. Jacobson for bringing the diary to my attention and for providing me with missing pages from the Hebrew University copy.

31. Amit Gish, "Ownerless Objects? The Story of the Books Palestinians Left behind in 1948," *Jerusalem Quarterly,* no. 33: 18.

32. Turjman diary, "Cinematographic Propaganda for the Ottoman Army," March 31, 1915: "waqafna fi bab al-khalil nantadhir qudum khalil al-sakaini la'anahu dhahaba ila ra'is al baladiiya yas'alahu bi'an yusa'id fi dif'i badalahu al-naqdi. Thumma hadara ubasharana ba'anna sayadfa' badalahu fi hadha al yawm, fasurra al-jami', thumma sirna wanahnu natajathab atraf al hadith." "We were all waiting for Khalil Sakakini to come to Jaffa Gate since he went to see the mayor, asking him to help in paying his military exemption fees *[badal].* Then he came and assured us that his *badal* will be paid today. Everybody was happy, and we proceeded on our walking and chatting."

33. Sakakini diary, vol. 2, 158–59 (emphasis added). This entry is dated March 28 and covers a ten-day period.

34. All data about Turjman's personal life, unless otherwise mentioned, come from his diary.

35. According to Saleh Turjman, Ihsan's nephew, the Turjmans, also known as the Salihs, were Asyad, tracing their origins to the family of Prophet Muhammad. In the eighteenth century they were challenged in the Court of Aleppo to produce evidence of this lineage, and upon producing a valid genealogy, they were allowed to continue bearing the title of Sayyids. Interview with Saleh Turjman, Ramallah, January 2006.

36. Hijjat Waqf Qasim Beyk Turjman, Islamic Court of Jerusalem, file no. 201, p. 130. I am grateful to Dr. Muhammad Ghosheh for providing me with this information about the properties of the Turjman family in the eighteenth and nineteenth centuries.

37. *Hijjat Waqf Ahmad Beyk al Turjman, 1735,* Islamic Court of Jerusalem, file no. 227, p. 289.

38. Most of this information comes from Huda Khalidi (Mrs. Abdul Shafie) and from Ihsan's grand-nephew Saleh Turjman (interviews in Ramallah in October 2004 and January 2005).

39. Even today, the road connecting the New Gate to Damascus Gate is still popularly known among the Jerusalem elderly as 'qbet al Manzil.

40. Omar Salih Barghouti, *Al Marahil, Tarikh Siyasi* (Beirut: Al Mu'assasah al Arabiyyah lil Dirasat wal Nashr, 2001), 154.

41. Ibid., 165.

42. Sarkis Boghosian. *Diary of an Armenian Officer in the Ottoman Army* [in Armenian]. 2 vols. (Paris: n.p., 1931). I am indebted to George Hintilian for bringing this diary to my attention.

43. Dahiliye Nezareti, Emniyet-Umumiye Mudiriyeti [Ministry of Interior, General Directorate], Evrak Numarsu [number of telegrams]: 4562–954, 8 Huzeiran, 1335 (June 1919).

44. Khalil Sakakini recorded Ihsan's death in the diaries he wrote while he was in his Damascus jail.

45. William Pfaff, *The Bullet's Song: Romantic Violence and Utopia* (New York: Simon and Schuster, 2005), cited by Pankaj Mishra, "A Cautionary Tale for Americans," *New York Review of Books,* May 26, 2005.

46. Turjman diary, "What Will Be the Fate of Palestine in This War?" 1.

47. Muhammad Izzat Darwazeh, *Mudhakkirat Muḥammad 'Izzat Darwazeh, 1305 H-1404 H/1887 M-1984 M: sijill ḥafil bi-masirat al-ḥarakah al-ʿArabiyah wa-al-qaḍiyah al-Filasṭiniyah khilala qarn min al-zaman,* vol. 1 (Beirut: Dar al-Gharb al-Islami. 1993), 258–59.

48. Fasih, *Diary,* 26.

49. Darwazeh, *Mudhakarat,* 260.

50. In the north, especially in Nablus, pro-Ottoman sentiments continued to be strong even after the Ottoman defeat in Jerusalem, and were articulated by figures such as Muhammad Izzat Darwazeh and Ihsan Nimr.

51. Najib Nassar, *Riwayat Miflih al-Ghassani* (Haifa: al-Karmil Press, 1922; Nazareth: al Sawt Publications, 1981). The 1981 edition, which is the one cited in later notes, has a long introduction by Hanna Abu Hanna and a useful glossary of terms. Abu Hanna makes clear that Miflih is a thinly disguised cover for Nassar himself—hence my use of the term Miflih/Nassar.

52. Ibid., 76, 246.

53. Ibid., 83–85.

54. Ibid., 47.

55. Ibid., 48.

56. Ibid., 49.

57. Anthony Bruce, *The Last Crusade: The Palestine Campaign in the First World War* (London, John Murray, 2003), 23–25; see also Hasan Kayali, *Arabs and Young Turks: Ottomanism, Arabism, and Islamism in the Ottoman Empire, 1908–1918* (Berkeley: University of California Press, 1997), 46.

58. Bruce, *The Last Crusade,* 19–22.

59. Kayali, *Arabs and Young Turks,* 189.

60. Ahmad Cemal Pasha, *Memoirs* (Arabic Edition) (Beirut: al Dar al Arabiyyah lil Mawsu'at, 2004), 187–88.

61. Quoted by Geoffrey Lewis, "An Ottoman Officer in Palestine, 1914–1918," in *Palestine in the Late Ottoman Period,* ed. David Kushner (Jerusalem, Yad Izhak Ben Zvi, 1986), 403.

62. Kayali, *Arabs and Young Turks,* 193; also Darwazeh, *Mudhakarat.*

63. For a detailed discussion of the southern boundaries of Palestine and the concept of Palestine's administrative boundaries at the end of World War I, see Gideon Biger, *An Empire in the Holy Land: Historical Geography of the British Administration in Palestine, 1917–1929* (New York: St Martin's Press, 1994), 39–44.

64. *Osmanli Atlasi,* ed. Rahmi Tekin and Yasar Bas (Istanbul: Osav, 2003), 112–13.

65. Ibid., 104–5, 120.

66. Muhammad Is'af Nashashibi, "al 'Arabiyyah al Misriyyah," in *Nuql al Adib* (Beirut: Dar Rihani, 1947), 161; originally published in Jerusalem 1352 (Hijri).

67. Hasan Ali Hallaq, ed., *Mudhakarrat Salim Ali Salam (1868–1938)* [The Memoirs of Salim Ali Salam] (Beirut: al Dar al jami'yyat, 1982), 127–28.

68. Ibid., 128.

69. Wajīh Kawtharānī, *Bilād al-Shām: al-sukkān, al-iqtiṣād, wa-al-siyāsah al-Faransīyah fī maṭla' al-qarn al-'ishrīn: qirā'ah fī al-wathā'iq* (Beirut: Ma'had al-Inmā' al-'Arabī, 1980), 256.

70. Sakakini, *Yawimiyat,* vol. 3, *The Mandate and Questions of Identity, 1919–1922,* (2004), 46.

71. Fasih, *Diary,* 133–34.

72. James Gelvin, *The Modern Middle East: A History* (London: Oxford University Press, 2005), 101.

73. "Arabic time probably has its roots in the common and most logical system of timekeeping used most places in the world until about A.D. 1600. In those days, daytime was divided into 12 equal parts, and nighttime also into 12 equal parts. Depending on the season, hours used in the daytime were either longer or shorter than hours used during the night. The sundials and astrolabes used as timekeepers were calibrated to divide into 12 regardless of the seasons. Thus, the same sundial could divide both a long summer daylight period and a short winter day equally into 12. The 'day' was made up of 24 hours and began at sunset. Twelve hours of darkness preceded 12 hours of daylight, although the hours in the daytime were not the same length as

the nighttime hours. This system of beginning the new 'day' at sunset remained in use on the isolated Arabian Peninsula when it became the practice in Europe to commence the 24-hour period not at dusk, as had theretofore been the custom, but in the middle of the nighttime part— and to end it in the middle of the following nighttime part. Thus, roughly speaking, six hours of darkness were followed by 12 hours of daylight and then six more hours of darkness to make the complete 24-hour period." From Elias Antar, "Dinner at When?" *Aramco Magazine,* March/April 1969, 2–3.

74. I am grateful to Saleh Turjman for this piece of information. (interview January 11, 2006, Ramallah). Ihsan studied in al-Dusturiyya; Adel and Hasan, at St George's College; and the three girls, Asma, Sirat, and Yusra, at the Sisters of Zion school. All schools in Jerusalem.

75. Yacoub Awdat, "Sheik Muhammad al Salih," in *A'lam al Fikr wal Adab fi Filasteen* (Jerusalem: Dar al Isra', 1992), 342–43.

76. Martin Strohmeier, "Al Kulliyya al-Salahiyya, A Late Ottoman University in Jerusalem," in *Ottoman Jerusalem: The Living City 1517–1917,* ed. Sylvia Auld and Robert Hillenbrand (London: Altajir World of Islam Trust, London, 2001), 57–62.

77. Ibid., 60.

78. Turjman diary. See the entries on May 5, 1915, "Adel Jaber Defends the Government"; and May 15, 1915, "Is Adel Effendi an Ottoman Spy?"

79. Ibid.

80. These are the expressions used by Muhammad Izzat Darwazeh in his memoirs and by Strohmeier ("Al Kulliyya al-Salahiyya"), who wrote from a different perspective but basically offered the same assessment of Cemal Pasha's objectives.

81. Strohmeier, "Al Kulliyya al-Salahiyya," 61.

82. Ibid.

83. Barghouti, *Al Marahil,* 187.

84. Sakakini diary, vol. 2, March 28, 1915, 158–59.

85. Falih Rıfkı [Atai], *Zeytindagi* (Istanbul: n.p., 1932; repr. Istanbul: Bates Yaymevi, 1981). I have relied here on Geoffrey Lewis's essay on Rıfkı, "An Ottoman Officer in Palestine, 1914–1918."

86. Ibid., 407–8.

87. Ibid., 405.

88. Ibid., 411.

89. Ibid., 412.

90. Ibid.

91. Ibid.

92. Ibid., 413.

93. Ibid., 414 (emphasis added).

94. John Berger, "An Article of Faith," in *About Looking* (New York: Vintage Books, 1991), 130.

95. Darwazeh, *Memoirs*.

96. "The Government Imposes a Locust Tax Is Imposed on the City's Residents," Turjman diary, Friday, April 23, 1915, 33–34.

97. See Wasif Jawharīyah, Salim Tamari, and Issam Nassar, *Al Quds al'Uthmaniyyeh fil Mudhakarat al Jawhariyyeh': al-kitāb al-awwal min mudhakkirāt al-mūīqī Wāṣif Jawharīyah, 1904–1917.* [Ottoman Jerusalem: 1904–1917] (Beirut: Mu'assasat al-Dirāsāt al-Filasṭīnīyah, 2003).

98. "Jerusalem Whores Celebrate the Anniversary of Sultan Mehmet Rashad," Turjman diary, Tuesday, April 27, 1915, 47–48.

99. "Teachers Bring in Prostitutes to Their Schools," Turjman diary, Wednesday, May 12, 1915, 72.

100. Ibid.

101. "An Encounter with a Prostitute," Turjman diary, Thursday, April 29, 1915, 50–51. A majidi was twenty piasters.

102. "When Commander Ruşen Bey Is Drunk, All Work Is Suspended," Turjman diary, Wednesday, April 28, 1915, 154.

103. "Veiling and the Status of Muslim Women," April 28, 1915, 155.

104. "Misfortunes Invade Us All at Once: War, Inflation, and Diseases," Turjman diary, Sunday, May 9, 1915, 68.

105. "Sherif Hussein Declares Rebellion against the State," Turjman diary, Monday, July 10, 1916, 181.

106. "I Am Ottoman by Name Only, the World Is My Country," Friday, September 10, 1915, 132.

107. Sakakini diary, 2003.

108. Hanssen, "Public Morality and Marginality," 189–95.

109. Ya'acov Yehoshua, *Yerushalaim Tmol Shilshom,* part 2 (Jerusalem: Rubin Mas, 1979), 33–36. I am grateful to Yair Wallach for this information.

110. Jawharīyah, Tamari, and Nassar, *Al Quds al 'Uthmaniyyeh fil Mudhakarat al Jawhariyyeh*.

111. Strategic marriages across regions existed earlier for upperclass and merchant families but were outside the capacities of ordinary citizens.

112. See Ami Ayalon, *Reading Palestine: Printing and Literacy, 1900–1948* (Austin: University of Texas Press, 2004).

113. Awdat, "Sheikh Muhammad al Salih."

114. Kamel Assali, *Muqaddima fi tarikh al-tibb fil-Quds* (Amman: University of Jordan Publications, 1994).

115. "I Was Not Touched by a Human," Turjman diary, Friday, September 10, 1915, 262.

116. For Palestine I was able to find three sets of love correspondence for that period: love letters between Khalil Sakakini and Sultana Abdo, Musa Alami's letters to his future wife from Aleppo Alia Jabiri, and the letters of Alphonse Alonzo to his fiancée, Afifeh Sidawi.

117. See Issam Nassar, *Laqaṭat mughayirah: al-taṣwir al-maḥalli al-mubakkir fi Filasṭin, 1850–1948* (London: Mu'assasat 'Abd al-Muḥsin al-Qaṭṭan, 2005).

118. Abu Khaldun Saṭi' Husri, *The Day of Maysalun: A Page from the Modern History of the Arabs,* trans. Sidney Glazer (Washington, D.C.: Middle East Institute, 1966).

119. In this chapter I use both names: Aref Shehadeh for the war period and Aref Aref (which he assumed after his return to Palestine) for his reflections in the postwar period.

120. Muhammad Muslih, *The Origins of Palestinian Nationalism* (New York: Columbia University Press, 1988).

121. Aref Aref, *Mujaz Siratuh 1892–1964* [an autobiographical essay published as a pamphlet] (Jerusalem: al Maaref Press, 1964); and Yacoub Awdat, *Min a'lam al-fikr wa-al-adab fi Filasṭin* (Amman: Wakalat al-Tawzi' al-Urduniyyah, 1987), 400–403.

122. Awdat, "Sheik Muhammad al Salih," 406.

123. The information about his early years comes from his *Mujaz Siratuh*.

124. Awdat, *Min a'lam al-fikr wa-al-adab fi Filastin*, 400. In *Ru'yaii*, he refers to al-Muntada in Istanbul as the forum "which we, Arabic speakers have established in Asetanah, and in which we took an oath to struggle for the freedom, unity and independence of our homeland" ([1918; Beirut: Dar al Rihan, 1957], 5; all page numbers refer to the 1957 edition, which was issued with a new introduction). For details about the ideology of the Arab Club in Istanbul, see Muslih, *The Origins of Palestinian Nationalism*.

125. Awdat, *Min a'lam al-fikr wa-al-adab fi Filastin*, 405.

126. Ibid., 400–401.

127. For a detailed discussion of Abdel Karim Khalil and debates with the Ottoman Decentralization Party and the Arab Club, see Suhaila Rimawi, "Pages from the History of Societies in Bilad al Sham 1908–1918," in *Al-Ḥarakah al-'Arabiyah al-qawmiyah fi mi'at 'am, 1875–1982*, ed. Naji 'Allush and Ibrahim Ibrash (Amman: Dar al-Shuruq, 1997), 120–23.

128. Aref, *Mujaz Siratuh*, 2–3. However, the major battle at Erzurum—in which the Russian forces, led by the Grand Duke Nicholas, decisively defeated the Ottomans—was fought on February 16, 1916. Aref may have been mistaken about the dates.

129. Aref, *Ru'yaii*.

130. Yücel Yanikdag, "Ottoman Prisoners of War in Siberia," *Journal of Contemporary History* 34, no. 1 (1999). On the high rate of camp deaths, see also Peter Gatrell, "Prisoners of War in the Eastern Front during World War I," *Kritika: Explorations in Russian and East Eurasian History* 6, no. 3 (Summer 2005): 562.

131. See ibid., 557–66.

132. Awdat, *Ru'yaii*, 4.

133. Ibid. The paper actually was a joint production with fellow officer Ahmad Kayyali.

134. These letters and postcards have been reprinted in Zvi Alexander, *Osmanlı sahra postaları: Filistin (1914–1918): Alexander Koleksiyonu* (Istanbul: Turkiye Ekonomik ve Toplumsal Tarih Vakfı, 2000).

135. Gatrell, "Prisoners of War" (emphasis added). Gatrell addresses only literature on German and Austro-Hungarian prisoners.

136. The expression was used by the Austrian writer Heimito von Doderer, quoted in ibid., 563.

137. Yanikdag, "Ottoman Prisoners of War in Siberia."

138. Gatrell, "Prisoners of War," 561.

139. Yanikdag, "Ottoman Prisoners of War in Siberia," 73.

140. Ibid., 77.

141. Ibid., 75.

142. Ibid., 74.

143. Ibid., 76–77.

144. Ibid., 77.

145. Aref Aref Photo Album and Diary (unpublished), in In'ash al Usra Library. As far a I know, only one issue of *Naqatu Allah,* no. 35, has survived.

146. Qur'an, Hod:45. For details on the Qur'anic story, see the al Ahsas website, www.ahsas.net/vb/showthread.php?t = 4611 (accessed September 1, 2008).

147. Yanikdag, "Ottoman Prisoners of War in Siberia," 77.

148. Awdat, *Min a'lam al-fikr wa-al-adab fi Filasṭin,* 401.

149. Al-Aref, *Mujaz Siratuh,* 3.

150. Awdat, *Ru'yaii,* 5. Aref attributes the news to a letter he received from Rashid Rida, editor of *AlManar* (Cairo). Rida informed him that several of his comrades from Istanbul days had joined Sherif Hussein and were involved in the siege of Medina.

151. Faridah Aref Amad, "Aref al Aref, My Father," *al Turath wal Mujtama',* no. 41, July 2005.

152. Ibid.

153. Gatrell, "Prisoners of War," 564.

154. Yanikdag, "Ottoman Prisoners of War in Siberia," 80.

155. Ibid.

156. Gatrell, "Prisoners of War," 564–65.

157. Ibid., 565.

158. On the impact of the revolution on internal dissension among prisoners, see ibid., 564.

159. Yanikdag, "Ottoman Prisoners of War in Siberia," 81.

160. Faridah Aref Amad describes the encounter in "Aref al Aref, My Father" 1.

161. Bayan Nuwayhid Hut, *Qiyadat wa-al-mu'assasat al-siyasiyah fi Filastin, 1917–1948* (Beirut: Mu'assasat al-Dirasat al-Filastiniyah, 1981), 86–87. See also Darwazeh, *Mudhakkirat Muḥammad 'Izzat Darwazeh*, vol. 1, 326.

162. Muslih, *The Origins of Palestinian Nationalism*.

163. Hut, *Qiyadat wa-al-mu'assasat al-siyasiyah fi Filastin*, 87.

164. Ibid., 86–89; Yehoshua Porath, *The Emergence of the Palestinian-Arab National Movement, 1918–1929* (London: Cass, 1974), 74–77.

165. See, for example, Aref's unsigned editorial "Nadhra ila al Ghad," *Surya al Janubiyyah* 1, no. 48 (March 26, 1920 [6 Rajab, 1338]).

166. Darwazeh, *Mudhakkirat*, 326–27. Darwazeh was probably referring to al Jam'iyya Arabiyya al Filastiniyah (Arab Palestinian Society), which was disseminating anti-Zionist materials in Damascus. See Porath, *The Emergence of the Palestinian-Arab National Movement*, 88.

167. Hut, *Qiyadat wa-al-mu'assasat al-siyasiyah fi Filastin*, 118.

168. Darwazeh, *Mudhakkirat*, 326.

169. Awdat, *Min a'lam al-fikr wa-al-adab fi Filastin*, 405.

170. Yanikdag, "Ottoman Prisoners of War in Siberia," 74.

171. Quoted by Elias Sahhab, "Sati al Husari: The Intellectual and the Activist," in Naji Allush, *The Arab National Movement in 100 Years*, 409 (emphasis added).

172. "Sabah erkenden uyandım. Bahçeye indim biraz dolaştım. Biraz da (çiçek) kopardım. Diğr bahçeye attım. Bir yemeklik fasülye topladım. Ben bahçede dolaşırken fikrimde hep sen vardın. Sensiz hiçbir şey güzel değil. Meğer bahçeyi güzelleştiren senmişsin. Meğer sensiz hiçbir şeyde lezzet yokmuş. Allah seni başımdan eksik etmesin. Bütün hayatımızı güzel eden sensin. Bizden ayrılırken biraz nezleydin. Onu düşünüyorum. Rica ederim bana sağlığınla ilgili bilgi ver. Seni bütün kalbiyle seven hayat arkadaşın." I am very grateful to Sibel Sayk and Muna Guvenc for providing the translation from Ottoman Turkish.

173. Jawharīyah, Tamari, and Nassar, *Al Quds al 'Uthmaniyyeh fil Mudhakarat al Jawhariyyeh'*, 139.

174. *Onbaşı* was an Ottoman military rank equivalent to lieutenant.

175. Communicated to me by his grandson, Dr. Sami Awad, Ramallah, July 16, 2006.

THE DIARY OF IHSAN TURJMAN

For ease of reading, I have added the headings in this excerpt of the diary, with the exception of "Today Is My Birthday," which is Ihsan Turjman's own heading. All translations from Arabic are mine.

1. I have used the Ottoman and Hijri calendars only in this first entry. All subsequent entries use the Gregorian calendar.

2. Khalil Sakakini (1878–1951) was an educator and essayist from Jerusalem. He founded al-Dusturiyya College, known for its progressive pedagogy, in 1909, and Ihsan studied there before the war. He was imprisoned by the Ottomans in 1917 because he came under suspicion for his nationalist activities. In 1918 he escaped from Damascus and joined the Arab rebellion in Hauran. Sakakini kept a diary, which is alluded to here. His daughter Hala published selections from his diary in 1951 (reprint; Khalil Sakakini, *Kadhā anā yā dunyā* [Beirut: al-Ittiḥād al-ʿĀmm lil-Kuttāb wa-al-Ṣuḥufīyīn al-Filasṭīnīyīn, al-Amānah al-ʿĀmmah, 1982]); hereafter Sakakini diary.

Hasan Khalidi (1893–1966) was a medical officer in the Fourth Imperial Army and Ihsan's confidant and cousin. Born in Jerusalem, he studied medicine at the American University in Beirut, where he received his degree in 1915. He became a medical officer in the Ottoman army and later the director of government hospitals in Nablus (1920) and Jaffa. Khalidi published several books of essays.

Omar Salih Barghouti was an advocate and Ottoman officer whose family owned the feudal estates of Deir Ghassaneh. After the war he became involved with the Defense Party. He wrote extensively on common law, and his diary was published posthumously; see Omar Salih Barghouti, *al-Marahil: Tarikh siyasi* [Turning Points: A Political History] (Beirut: al-Mu'assasa al-ʿArabiyya li al-dirasat wa al-nashr, 2001).

3. Ali Ruşen Bey, the commander of the Jerusalem Garrison, fought

against the British in the battle of Jerusalem (December 1917), withdrew to Anatolia with his troops, and was decorated for leading the resistance against Greek occupation after the war.

4. Newspapers were suspended during the first two years of the war. Telegraphic bulletins and rumors became the main sources of news from the front.

5. A *matleek* was a small coin in the Ottoman currency, a fraction of a piaster.

6. For a payment of 50 Ottoman pounds, certain categories of the population, such as teachers, could receive exemption from military service.

7. Nebi Musa was a public festival celebrating the birth of the Prophet Moses. It grew out of the twelfth-century practices of Sultan Salah ed-Din Ayyubi (Saladin) after his capture of Jerusalem from the Crusaders. The annual spring event was one of the most popular Muslim holidays in Palestine and also involved Christian and Jewish participation. Celebrants carrying regional banners started the procession to the feast in Jerusalem and walked to the shrine of Moses, which Muslim tradition places near Jericho. In the Jewish tradition, the location of the tomb of Moses is unknown, because he died near Mt. Nebo in Transjordan before reaching the Holy Land.

8. It is not clear why these women were being harassed by the police. But the entry on April 1 indicates that during the period of the Nebi Musa festival (which started at the Haram compound) the authorities were getting nervous that nationalist and antiwar elements would use the festivities as a cover for their protests.

9. Western time was known as *franji* time. It differed from Arabic time, which was based on the sundial and was calculated by the solar cycle. Ihsan used both times, as well as three calendars, in his diary.

10. The Egyptian campaign was going badly, and the Ottoman army had to remove public decorations previously put up in anticipation of a victory over the British in the Canal Zone.

11. Ihsan is referring to the infamous labor battalions *(Tawabeer al 'amaleh)*. The Fourth Army Command in Damascus was not sure of the loyalty of Palestinian and Syrian Christians and Jews and hesitated to

include them in combat positions, suspecting that they might secretly sympathize with the British war efforts.

12. When Khalil Sakakini established al-Dusturiyya College, he not only sought to introduce his progressive methods of education into the private sector, but he was also intent on creating an alternative to missionary education. Ihsan was secretly infatuated Khalil's wife, Sultana, as will become obvious from his coded entries in this diary.

13. Milia Sakakini was Khalil's sister and a teacher at al-Dusturiyya College.

14. Ihsan does not identify Lady T or A.B. From the context, however, we can guess that A.B. is either Adel Jaber or Is'af Nashashibi, both of whom he disliked intensely.

15. The Garbage Battalion was one of the labor battalions, established to put people to work collecting garbage in lieu of military service. Like the other labor battalions, the so-called garbage battalions were volunteer companies in name only. Older people and minorities were conscripted in them either because they were deemed unfit for combat duty or because they were not trusted to serve at the front.

16. Hanim (Khanum) was a Turkish title of respect for upper- and middle-class women. This form of address was widely used in the Arab world in this period.

17. The Fourth Army was preparing a second attack on the Suez Canal.

18. Manshiyyeh was the municipal garden and café on Jaffa Road, near the Russian compound. The name of the band, Shami, indicates that it was possibly visiting from Damascus.

19. Hasan Khalidi was Ihsan's maternal cousin and a military officer in the Fourth Army.

20. The fight against locusts had so far been carried out by farmers, who destroyed the insects' eggs before they could incubate. Ihsan is referring to a debate about whether the government should now mobilize ordinary citizens against the locusts as well.

21. Eighty-five piasters was an ordinary soldier's salary, slightly less than one Ottoman pound (one hundred piasters).

22. One French pound was equivalent to 90 Ottoman piasters.

23. The full name of the paper is *al Himara al Qahira* (the Stubborn Donkey). It was founded in September 1911 as a literary satirical publication, published in Haifa, and edited by Khalil Zakkout and Najib Jana. See Yusif Khoury, *The Arabic Press in Palestine 1876–1948* (Beirut: Institute of Palestine Studies, 1986), 21.

24. Tal'at, Enver (Anwar), and Cemal Pashas were the three leaders of the Young Turks in the Committee of Union and Progress. Tal'at at this time was the minister of the interior and later (in 1917) became the grand vizier; Enver was the minister of war, and Cemal was the minister of the navy and the military governor of Syria during the war years.

25. Tetley Sirt was a brand of first-class Ottoman cigarettes made in Istanbul.

26. Hafeer and Ibin were Ottoman military posts near Beer Sheva and Areesh (in Sinai). Both had military airports.

27. The wording does not make clear whether the order was not carried out for bureaucratic reasons or because of resistance.

28. The British and French had imposed a blockade against all shipments to the Syrian coast during the war, which was a major factor in inducing the famine of 1916–17. Within Palestine the famine was compounded by three successive years of drought (1914–1916) and by the conscription of peasants and their animals. Thanks to Roger Owen for alerting me to these added factors.

29. Cemal Pasha the Little *(Küçük),* known as Mersini, was the commander of the Eighth Army.

30. Ibin was an advanced military outpost and airport in Sinai.

31. These men were active figures in the Arabist movement during the war period. Mughrabi was an editor of both *al Sharq* newspaper in Damascus and *Burhan* newspaper in Tripoli. Haj Amin was then an officer in the Ottoman army serving in the Black Sea and later became the mufti of Jerusalem. Nashashibi was a leading poet and essayist and a close associate of Sakakini at al-Dusturiyya College.

32. Abdo was an Islamic reformer and associate of Jamal Din Afghani. Qasim Amin was the author of *The Liberation of Women* (Cairo, 1901) and an advocate of educating women in Egypt and the Arab East. For an English translation of the book, see Amin, *The Liberation of*

Women; and, The New Woman: Two Documents in the History of Egyptian Feminism (Cairo: American University in Cairo Press, 2000).

33. These are Ottoman fiscal years and refer to men in their forties, who were so far exempt from service—hence the invocation of God's mercy.

34. Notre Dame was a French Catholic building opposite the New Gate. It was confiscated as enemy property and became the military headquarters of the Commissariat. Cemal Pasha's headquarters was the Augusta Victoria Hospital in the Mount of Olives.

35. Hilmi Effendi Husseini was born in Jerusalem in 1890, studied at St. George, and worked in the civil service, most notably in the land registry in 1921. He was later the district governor of several cities, including Haifa.

36. Tariq Ben Ziad was a commander of the Muslim army that conquered Spain in 732 A.D.

37. Rustum Haydar (1889–1925) was a leader of the Arabist movement at the end of the Ottoman era. Of Lebanese origin from the town of Baalbak, he studied at the Rashidiyyah School in Baalbak and the Imperial School in Istanbul. He received his advanced training in history and politics in Paris. He founded the Young Arab Society with Awni Abdul Hadi and taught at al-Salahiyya College in Jerusalem and Damascus. In 1917 he deserted the Ottomans and joined the rebel army of Prince Faisal, eventually becoming Prince Faisal's private secretary. He participated in most of the peace conferences after the war in which the fate of the Arab regions was decided. (See Muhammad R. Haydar and Naǧda F. Ṣafwa, *Muḏakkirat Rustum Ḥaidar* [The Memoirs of Rustum Haydar], edited by Najdah Safwat (Beirut: ad-Dār al-'Arabīya lil-Mausū'āt, 1988).

38. Jamal Husseini was a Jerusalemite leader of the movement for the independence of Palestine. He studied medicine at the American University in Beirut and joined the Ottoman army in 1914. Husseini was appointed to the Higher Islamic Council in Jerusalem during the British Mandate. In 1934 he was elected secretary of the Arab Executive Council. He founded the Palestine Arab Party in 1935 and was elected as party chairman. Imprisoned three times by the British authorities, he was exiled from Palestine from 1941 to 1946. Upon

his return he resumed leadership of the party until the war of 1948, when he went into exile again. (See Ahmad Khalil Aqqad, *Mann Huwa fi Rijalat Filistin fi Fatrat al Intidab* [Who Is Who in Palestine?] (Jaffa: Maktab al Sahafa wal Nashr, 1946), 34–35.

39. Expressing these sentiments against Cemal would surely have exposed the writer to great danger, since the Jerusalem police was busy looking for seditious literature in private homes in the old city. Sakakini, for example, wrote that he used to hide his diary every day after making his entries, even though his oppositional sentiments were much milder. Ihsan never left his diary at work (Commissariat) and kept it hidden at home.

40. The word *Shami* (Syrian) here includes the Palestinian soldiers, as is clear from the following sentence.

41. Before the Balkan War (1912) and World War I, non-Muslim Ottomans, especially Jews and Christians, paid an exemption tax *(jizya)* in lieu of service in the army. After the Constitutional Reform of 1908, the legal category of *dhimmi* was abolished, and non-Muslims were conscripted on a wide scale beginning with the Crimean War.

42. This book was apparently a marriage manual. Cheap editions of such books were available in Palestine and Syria during World War I. It is unlikely that Ihsan was reading the book in English; he had an Arabic translation.

43. Mammilla, formally known as Ma'manallah, is the main Muslim cemetery in Jerusalem.

44. The Khalidyyeh, which is still open today, is an old manuscript library near the Magharbeh compound at the entrance to the Haram.

45. Nebi Samuel, a village north of Jerusalem, was a strategic location where some of the most ferocious battles of World War I were fought around Jerusalem in 1917.

46. Faidi Alami (1865–1924) had been the mayor of Jerusalem (1906–9) and the representative of the Jerusalem district in the Ottoman parliament in 1914. He was apparently related to one of the teachers. See Adel Mana, *A'lām Filasṭīn fī awākhir al-'ahd al-'Uthmānī* [Palestine Notables at the End of the Ottoman Era] (Beirut: Mu'assasat al-Dirāsāt al-Filasṭīnīyah, 1995), 287. The amount of 150 qirsh is equivalent to 1.5

Ottoman pound—in that period twice the monthly salary of a foot soldier.

47. *Al Zamakhshari* is a classical work of religious interpretation. Zamakhshari was a Mu'tazalite and a free thinker.

48. Both Sakakini and Sultana's name are written in code, and Sultana's name is unusually capitalized (that is, written as Al-Sultana in Arabic). This sentence is rather obscure, and the fact that Ihsan coded the names suggests that Ihsan had a crush on Sultana Abdo (Khalil's wife), who was newly married to his teacher. I am grateful to Zakariyya Muhammad, who was able to break Ihsan's coded entries and provide me with the key.

49. The coded name here is Sakakini.

50. "In a few years," refers to after the end of the war, when he would have the opportunity to get married.

51. Karm al A'raj is an area in Musrara, north of the old city where the Turjmans had their properties. The family moved there in the 1920s, after Ihsan's death.

52. As'ad Shuqairi represented the Acre region in Istanbul. He was a leading supporter of the CUP and Cemal Pasha in particular. In 1916 he achieved notoriety for issuing a religious decree legitimizing the hanging of Arab nationalists in Beirut as traitors to the Ottoman state. His son Ahmad became the chairman of the Palestine Liberation Organization in 1964.

53. "The Straits" likely refers to the Dardanelles or Sea of Marmara.

54. Enver Pasha (1881–1922) was the war minister and a leader of the CUP. He was killed in battle at the Russian front in 1922, not in the way Turjman describes here.

55. Ihsan later wrote "lies" in the margin of this page.

56. No evidence exists that Adel Jaber was an Ottoman spy, as Turjman claims, so this comment may simply be an expression of his personal animosity toward Jaber. He may have believed that Jaber was competing with him for the affections of his beloved Thurayya. A contemporary compendium on Ottoman intelligence in Syria and Palestine does not mention Adel Jaber. See Aziz Bey, *Intelligence and Espionage in Lebanon, Syria, and Palestine during World War I* [an Arabic translation from Ottoman Turkish] (Beirut: Dar al Nahar, 1937). Aziz

Bey was the head of Ottoman intelligence in Damascus. However, Jaber, who was a member of Sakakini's inner circle, was known as a fierce defender of the Ottoman regime and a close associate of Cemal Pasha. In this he was not alone. In 1915 Cemal appointed him as a lecturer at al-Salahiyya College, at a time when the expressed aim of the college was to prepare young Arabs to be a loyal cadre in the Ottoman civil service. See Yacoub Awdat, *Min a'lām al-fikr wa-al-adab fī Filastīn* (Amman: Wakālat al-Tawzī' al-Urdunīyah, 1987), 85–87.

57. Baq'a was a southern neighborhood in Jerusalem, on the outskirts of Bethlehem.

58. Elsewhere in the diary Ihsan says that he was told that, as a soldier without means, he was unlikely to be accepted by Thurayya's family as a prospective suitor, even though her mother was favorable to his intentions.

59. Tawfiq Canaan was a doctor and officer in the Ottoman army, originally from Beit Jala. He later became a well-known dermatologist, trained in Berlin, who specialized in leprosy. In the 1920s he became the head of the Palestine Oriental Society and editor of its journal. He was the head of the Ottoman Military Hospital in Jerusalem; the head of the Leprosarium (a facility for lepers) in Talbieh, and the head of the Augusta Victoria hospital. He wrote numerous monographs and articles on peasant ethnography, articles on popular medicine, and scholarly medical treatises.

60. Haj Rashid Nashashibi was a Jerusalem notable and a member of the Ottoman City Council. He made a great fortune selling grain and other provisions to the Ottoman armed forces stationed in Palestine. He founded the Nashashibi neighborhood in Sheikh Jarrah and built a palatial mansion that later became the residence of the mayor, his son Ragheb. In the 1960s this mansion was demolished to make way for the current Ambassador Hotel. Readers can find the deleted entries in Tamari, *'Am al-Jarad*.

61. Several entries between May and September have been deleted.

62. In the first instance the diarist uses the term *al-Umma al Suriyyah* (the Syrian nation) indicating the whole of the Arab Levant. In the second mention of the region, he refers to the "Syrian and Palestinian countries."

63. Turjman is referring to the formation of the Ottoman Decentralization Party *(Hizb al-LaMarkaziyyah al 'Uthmani)* in 1912—an action that had the encouragement of the Egyptian authorities. Cairo at the time was a main center for Arab nationalist oppositional groups from the Syrian Ottoman provinces.

64. The most important of these groups, besides the Decentralization Party, were the Young Arab Society (al Arabiyya al Fatat), and the 'ahd group (the Covenant). The former was founded in Paris in 1909 by Abdel Ghani 'Araysi. The 'ahd group was established in October 1913 in Istanbul by Abdul Aziz Masri and was in close contact with the clandestine military organization within the Ottoman armed forces known as al Jam'iyya al Qahtaniyyah (the Qahtani Society). Hasan Kayyali claims that Masri was able to recruit a large number of Arab officers in the capital and that he had followers in Baghdad, Musil in addition to 'ahd branches in Lebanon, Syria, and Palestine. See Hasan Kayali, *Arabs and Turks 1908–1918: Ottomanism, Arabism, and Islamism in the Ottoman Empire, 1908–1918* (Berkeley: University of California Press, 1997), 123–25.

65. Sofar was the headquarters of the Ottoman Military Administration in Mount Lebanon.

66. Rida Solh was the deputy to the Ottoman Parliament from Beirut. His son, Riad Beyk Solh (1898–1951), was a nationalist figure during the war and later became the prime minister of Lebanon.

67. Abdul Ghani Araysi was a founder of the Young Arab Society in Paris (1909) and one of the Arab nationalist figures hanged by Cemal Pasha in Martyrs Square in Beirut in August 1915. Shibly Shmayyil was a Lebanese socialist and Darwinist intellectual. He was condemned to death by an Ottoman court for his nationalist activities but escaped to Egypt.

68. The expression "I am an Ottoman by name—my country is the world" was often used by Ihsan's mentor Khalil Sakakini. See Sakakini diary, vol. 2.

69. This is the only entry in the diary that starts with a Jerusalem notation.

70. Ihsan probably chose Switzerland because the country was neutral during the war.

71. Dhaheriyyeh lies south of Hebron and north of Beersheva. The seven-hour travel time is by horse.

72. Such a gift might be considered a bribe for having his name removed from the list.

73. Hussein Fakhri Khalidi, the brother of Hasan, was Ihsan's maternal cousin and, like his brother, a medical officer in the Ottoman army.

74. The word *mu'ashara* is crossed out in the diary. It is not clear what Turjman means, because the Arabic word could mean "sexual cohabitation" or "social companionship."

75. Thurayya's coded name is 'Antharaq, which translates from his code book as Ni'mati. Ihsan's younger brother married a woman called Ni'mati, but family sources indicate this is probably not the same woman, since Ihsan was killed in 1916 or 1917, and Aref Turjman did not marry until the late 1920s, when the "second" Ni'mati was in her early twenties. (Interview with Saleh Turjman, 2006).

76. Ihsan was hesitant about marrying Thurayya/Ni'mati –whom he knew from childhood—because she apparently was spoiled and had no knowledge of house management. All his hesitations evaporated when he saw her face unveiled four months before this entry.

77. The new Greek prime minister, Eleftherios Venizelos, was known for his sympathies with the Entente.

78. During World War I, the Jerusalem ratl was equivalent to 3000 grams (3 kilograms).

79. An Ottoman majidi was equivalent to 20 piasters. A soldier's salary was 85 piasters per month, making rice an expensive purchase.

80. Most Jerusalem households at the turn of the century baked their own bread in neighborhood ovens; buying baked bread was exceptional.

81. Ihsan turned twenty-three on this day by the Ottoman calendar. His birth was recorded on 17 Kanun Thani 1309 Ottoman, 1310 by the Hijri calendar.

82. The Capitulations, granting commercial privileges to Western powers in the Ottoman Empire, were not annuled until the Treaty of Sèvres in 1923. So either Ihsan is mocking the government here, or he

is referring to the abolition of Allied governments' postal privileges at the commencement of the war. Before this time, all major European powers maintained postal offices in Jaffa and Jerusalem. During the war, all mail was confined to the official Ottoman Post.

83. Fredrick Kress von Kressennstein was the commander of the Eighth Army.

84. The German Colony was the templar neighborhood of Haifa, which was on the southern slopes of Mt. Carmel facing the sea. It isn't clear whether the British targeted the neighborhood as a German target or whether they hit it accidentally.

85. al-Salahiyya College, at Saint Anne, was established in 1915 by Ahmad Cemal Pasha as a higher institute of learning for Arab and Muslim civil service.

86. As'ad Shuqairi was the deputy from Akka at the Ottoman parliament. He was a leading Palestinian supporter of the CUP and the war effort, as well as mufti (chief chaplain) of the Fourth Army. He became notorious for issuing a fatwa supporting the execution of the Arab nationalists in Beirut as traitors of the state.

87. The main purpose of the Hijaz visit was to mobilize support for the war among the Hijazi tribesmen and to consolidate the relationship with Sherif Hussein and the Hashemite leadership. Enver and Cemal (as became clear from the latter's memoirs) were aware that Sherif Hussein was secretly plotting with the British in Cairo against the Ottomans.

88. The mufti of Jerusalem was Sheikh Kamil Husseini, brother of Haj Amin Husseini.

89. Aziz Effendi Daudi was a lawyer and judge born in Jerusalem in 1890. He was appointed court clerk in the central court of Jerusalem during the Ottoman era and promoted to head clerk in the appeals court in Jaffa. After the Ottoman defeat in Jerusalem, he moved with the Ottoman administration to Nazareth and became the chief prosecutor in northern Palestine. During the Mandate period he became a judge in the higher appeals court. He presided over the case of Sultan Abdul Hamid's private property in Palestine during British colonial rule (Aqqad, *Rijalat Filastin fi fatrat al Intidab,* 48–49). In addition

to Ottoman state land, which was taken over by the British Mandate authority, substantial plots were registered in the name of the Sultan himself, which became a subject of litigation in the 1920s and 1930s.

90. There is a discrepancy between in the date of this entry and the time of the incident. Ihsan apparently recorded the events after he made the entry date here.

91. He is probably referring to the hospital of St. Louis, on Jaffa Road.

92. Both the Hijazi tribes and Sherif Hussein were paid an annual subsidy by Istanbul to protect the Haj routes. After the establishment of the Hijazi railroad, many tribes were no longer in great demand to provide services to pilgrims, and they also lost the business of the trade caravans that had once passed through on their way from Syria to Hijaz.

93. Arna'uti is an archaic Arabic word for Albanian that was commonly used in the Ottoman period. In the diary, Ihsan identified the officer as "Turkish Albanian."

94. The Turjman home was inside the Haram compound, but it had an external door that opened to Bab al Silsilah [Chaines] street. At night, access from the Haram area was locked, but people could enter from the street side. The house still exists.

95. This request may indicate that Rustum Effendi was a tenant on their property.

INDEX

Abdo, Muhammad, 40, 42, 110, 177n32

Abdo, Sultana, 99, 100 *fig9*, 121, 170n116, 176n12, 180n48

Abdülhamid, Sultan, 29, 36, 68, 184–85n89

Abu Ghazaleh, Rustum, 147

Abu Hanna, Hanna, 166n51

Abul Sa'ud, Abdul Salam, 149–53

Abul Su'ud, Mufti Taher, 28, 137

Abul Su'ud family, 21, 77

Adhm, Haqqi Bey, 131

Agati (Mersini soldier), 15

al-'ahd group, 27, 46, 182n64

al-Ahram, 131

airplanes, 106, 130

Alami, Faidi, 54, 121, 179n46

Alami, Musa, 39, 41, 42, 99, 170n116

Alami, Zuhdi, 120–21

Alami family, 77

Albanians, 11

alcohol, 109–10

Aleppo, 11, 140, 142; Court of, 165n35

Alexandria (Egypt), 10, 31

Allenby, Edmund, 24

Alonzo, Alphonse, 170n116

American Colony (Jerusalem), 119

Amin, Qasim, 43, 54–55, 110, 177–78n32

Anatolia, 43, 82, 115, 135

al-Aqsa Mosque (Jerusalem), 95, 96 *fig8*

Arab Club, 77–79

Arab East, 3, 5, 8, 77, 86. *See also* Palestine, Ottoman; Syria, Ottoman; *specific place*

Arab Enlightenment, 39

Arab Executive Council, 178n38

Arabic language, 115

Arabic time, 37–38, 167–68n73, 175n9

Arabism/Arabists: ODP and, 27; Shehadeh and, 68, 77–79, 82; significant figures, 177n31, 178n37. *See also* Arab nationalism/ nationalists

Arab Legion, 18

Arab modernity, 3, 5, 85

Ottoman Corps of Army Engineers, 10
Ottoman Decentralization Party (ODP), 27, 29, 69–70, 81, 182n63
Ottoman Empire: bureaucracy in, 92; calendar notations in, 37; censorship in, 43; constitutional revolution (1908), 3–4, 40, 69, 81, 86, 179n41; decentralization of, 41, 44, 69, 87; education in, 40; ethnic identity in, 15, 48–50; historical revision of, 5; impact of WWI on, 3–4, 5–12, 6 *fig1;* political activists in, 63–65; postal service in, 183–84n82; Second Constitutional Period, 65; subaltern chronicles of, 25. *See also* Palestine, Ottoman; Syria, Ottoman
Ottoman identity, loss of, 43–50, 63
Ottomanism, 65, 76, 81–85
Ottoman Military Administration, 182n65
Ottoman Parliament, 182n66
Ottoman Turkish language, 84

Palestine, Mandate, 4, 63–64, 67, 80–81, 88, 184–85n89
Palestine, Ottoman: Arabist movement in, 27; British blockade of, 51, 109, 177n28; British bombardment of, 123; British control of, 35, 104–5; decentering of, 32–34, 33 *fig4;* education in, 39–43; Egyptian annexation of, as future possibility, 26–35, 51, 87, 91–92; Egyptian influences on, 34; impact of WWI on, 8, 10–12, 51–56, 87–88, 177n28; mass deportations from, 48; modernity of, 35, 115; nationalist movement in, 182n64; post-WWI factions in,

28 *fig3;* press in, 59, 177n23; Syrian union with discussed, 35, 77; timekeeping methods in, 35–38; Turkish identity in, 50. *See also specific place*
Palestine Arab Party, 178–79n38
Palestine Liberation Organization (PLO), 180n52
Palestine Oriental Society, 181n59
Palestine Secret Society, 79–80
Palestinian Arab Society, 80
pan-Islamic movement, 42, 43
Pannekoek, Anton, 7
Paris (France), 131
pauperization, 4, 52
peasants: conscription into labor battalions, 8–11, 177n28; military impounding of grain from, 51, 177n28; urban migration of, 7–8, 9–10
Petro, Jurgi (George), 95, 99–102, 108, 112
Pfaff, William, 26
photography, 61
physical training classes, 59
police brutality, 95
political activism, 63–65
polygamy, 127
Porath, 78
postal service, 10, 183–84n82
press, 57
propaganda, 94–95, 106, 130, 141
prostitution, 7, 11, 53–54, 93, 112, 114, 120–21
protests, 155, 175n8

Qadri, Ahmad, 41
al-Quds al Sharif, Mutasarrıflık of, 4, 33 *fig4*
Qur'anic education, 39
Quttaineh family, 123
Quwakgi, Fawzi, 25

suspended during, 175n4; Palestinian factions following, 28 *fig3;* soldiers' diaries kept during, 3, 4–5, 85–88; timekeeping methods following, 36; totalizing effects of, 5–7, 51–56, 161–62n4; transformative effects of, 7–12, 57–58, 87–88, 162n4; Turkish/Arab loyalty during, 14
wrestling, amateur, 59

Ya'coubi, Salim, 28
Yanikdag, Yücel, 70, 72–75, 76, 82
Yehoshua, Ya'acov, 58

yellow fever, 140
YMCA, 73
Young Arab Society, 178n37, 182nn64, 67
Young Turks, 41, 177n24. *See also* Committee of Union and Progress (CUP)

Zakkout, Khalil, 177n23
Zamakhshari, 42–43, 180n47
Zeytindagi (Rıfkı), 50
Ziad, Tariq Ben, 113, 178n36
Zionism, 35, 77, 87, 104
Zureik, Nakhleh, 39

Text: 10/15 Janson

Display: Janson

Compositor: BookMatters, Berkeley

Indexer: Kevin Millham